SCIENCE AND CULTURE SERIES
JOSEPH HUSSLEIN, S.J., Ph.D., GENERAL EDITOR

SAVING ANGEL

VISION OF JOAN OF ARC — J. BASTIEN LEPAGE
Courtesy The Metropolitan Museum of Art, N. Y.

SAVING ANGEL

The Truth About Joan of Arc and the Church

By

Thomas
T. LAWRASON RIGGS

Late Spiritual Counsellor of Students
at Yale University and
Associate Fellow of Calhoun College,
Yale University

THE BRUCE PUBLISHING COMPANY
MILWAUKEE

Nihil obstat: Rev. H. B. Ries, Censor librorum
Imprimatur: ✠ Moyses E. Kiley, Archiepiscopus Milwaukiensis

November 5, 1943

TO THE MEMORY
OF
MY BROTHER

CONTENTS

PREFACE BY THE GENERAL EDITOR

WE have waited long for a book that should take up for us and unravel the tangled skein of controversy that still involves the judicial trials of the Maid of Orleans, a book that can be fascinating as it is convincing. Though concerned with plots and courts and documentary evidence, the story here told reveals to us in all its simplicity of appeal the heroic central figure of Joan of Arc — so young, so brave, so loyal, so truly maiden hearted, and withal so wise in her replies as to confound the deepest cunning of her adversaries.

Nor was there one trial only, but rather a whole succession of trials, before her death, after it, and even in our own day when, almost five centuries later, she was raised to the honors of the altar by that Church to whose head on earth she had in vain demanded that her case should be appealed.

The great mystery story of all history we may well call the particular phase of Joan's life treated in this book. But connected closely with her trials there quickly pass before us here the peaceful days at Domrémy spent in shepherding her flock; the breathless moments when she listened to celestial voices whose prophetic words were fulfilled in every syllable; her marches and her hardships and her battles in what seemed to be a hopeless cause; her glorious victory ending in the crowning of her king; and finally, her capture, no less clearly predicted, and her pathetic death by "fagot, stake, and torch," with the name of Jesus as the last word uttered by her lips.

Once more, it might appear, hell had triumphed, as when Christ hung dead upon the Cross. But for Him there was to be a Resurrection, and for her a Rehabilitation and a Canonization. And yet, in spite of all this vindication, and to clear up much newly caused modern bewilderment, there is great reason for this admirably written book.

But more than this. With Edna St. Vincent Millay we cannot help but turn to her, and in pleading words adjure her:

> Have no voices spoken plain:
> France has need of you again?

France? Most assuredly; but not France alone! All the world has need of her — not for the crowning now of a mere earthly monarch, but for the winning of mankind's due and rightful recognition to be given in this hour of distress to the one sole King of all the ages. Of what avail are battles fought and victories won and treaties signed, if He is not enthroned in the hearts, the minds, and the lives of men, as King of kings and Lord of lords? He alone can be our Peace.

And here a final word of tribute to the author of this book. In quick succession *Finis* has been written both to his noble volume and to his devoted, scholarly life. In his defense of what is right and good and pure his priestly heart beat high while writing these pages, and his trust in God was firm with the fortitude that he admired in the Maid of Orleans. He has fallen into the hands of a better Judge and One in whom his heart delighted.

JOSEPH HUSSLEIN, S.J., PH.D.,
General Editor, Science and Culture Series

AUTHOR'S FOREWORD

OF the making of books about St. Joan of Arc there is no end. The astounding career of this girl, who was leading troops into battle when she was seventeen years old, and, after remarkable military successes, was captured, tried, and executed soon after she was nineteen, has been dealt with by poets and historians, good, bad, and indifferent, of every tribe and nation under heaven, by believers and skeptics, by military experts, learned priests, and romantic ladies.

Every aspect of her life, every fact, circumstance, or tradition, remotely relating to her and to everyone connected with her, has been made the subject of patient research and the theme of countless monographs. St. Thérèse of Lisieux showed her devotion to Joan by a series of poems, from one of which the title of this book is taken. She has been portrayed, by Anatole France, as a weak-minded tool of priests, and by Jehanne d'Orliac — after the bewildering statement that "so far Joan of Arc has been approached from one point of view only" — as the pawn of the Dauphin's mother-in-law. Schiller imagined for her a death on the field of battle. It has been elaborately argued that she was the illegitimate daughter of the Duke of Orleans, that she was not burned at Rouen, that she was a spiritualistic medium. A certain Abbé Misset wrote a series of pamphlets to prove that Domrémy, her birthplace, was in Champagne rather than Lorraine. And all these elaborate theories have been elaborately refuted.

What remains to be said after piety and scholarship, not to mention prejudice and fantasy, have so voluminously said their say? Why should this mass of literature, in which so many admirable works are to be found, be increased by another? From the present writer's viewpoint the answer is a simple one. As a Catholic I am particularly interested in the question of St. Joan's relations with the Church. Now there is a great deal of material specially devoted to this subject in French, notably the massive studies of Canon Dunand and Father Ayroles; but these works are hard to find, and, because of their prolixity, almost as hard to read. In English I know of nothing at all adequate. Yet surely there is great interest in the subject among English-speaking Catholics, especially since the thesis of Joan's "Protestantism" has been so widely popularized by Mr. Bernard Shaw — though he did not, as we shall see, originate it.

It was Shaw's play which first made me wonder, as many other Catholics must have wondered, whither a thorough investigation of his thesis might lead. Was Joan really a heretic? Was she honestly and legally tried and condemned? Was the rehabilitation of 1456 really as worthy of ridicule as Mr. Shaw would have us believe? Must the Church accept Mr. Shaw's patronizing congratulations for having canonized in 1920 an ultra-Protestant martyr whom she had burned in 1431?

Investigation of these questions has led to the writing of the present book. It does not profess to be another biography of St. Joan, for which the reader must go elsewhere. If he is pressed for time, he may choose Hilaire Belloc. If he has plenty of time, and knows French, he cannot do better than read Gabriel Hanotaux. If he is content with history in the form of fiction, he will enjoy Mark Twain.

Furthermore, this book will avoid controversy concerning the voices and visions which inspired Joan's mission, though it will have many occasions to allude to them. Such controversy, besides being outside my scope, would be wasted on those who refuse to consider any evidence for the miraculous; while for others it is unnecessary.

The subject which this book does propose to discuss, if not exhaustively, at least clearly, is that of Joan's relations with the doctrinal and disciplinary authority of the Catholic Church. It will also consider the Church's judgment on these relations after Joan's death. Other matters will be dealt with only in so far as they seem relevant to the main theme, or necessary for its elucidation.

"That our present judgment may proceed from the face of God, who is the weigher of spirits, and who alone knoweth His revelations perfectly and judgeth them most truly, who breatheth where He will, and often chooseth the weak that He may confound the mighty . . ."

— Decree of Rehabilitation of
Joan of Arc
1456

1

THE SOURCES OF INFORMATION

JULES QUICHERAT, as part of his great edition of the trial and rehabilitation of St. Joan, published in 1847 no less than forty-three extracts dealing with Joan at considerable length, besides seven shorter references, from chroniclers and historians of the fifteenth century. These French, Burgundian, and foreign chroniclers are of varying degrees of importance and trustworthiness; but the interesting thing is, that if none of them had ever written, we would still know a great deal about the Maid of Orleans. Indeed, for the purposes of this book, we would know very nearly as much as we do now. For we would still have abundant information of a sort more direct than the chroniclers can give us, consisting of Joan's own utterances and of the sworn testimony of men and women who knew her. It is contained in the records of the Rouen trial (or, more exactly, trials) of 1431, and of the rehabilitation, which may be said to have started with a royal investigation in 1450, was formally taken over by the Church in 1455, and was completed in 1456. The character of these documents is of such uniquely absorbing interest, and acquaintance with them is so necessary for my subject, that they need to be discussed in some detail.

For much of our knowledge concerning the recording of the Rouen trial and the persons involved we depend on testimony given at the rehabilitation. Whenever this seems to be questionable, the fact will be duly noted.

There were three *greffiers* or recorders at the Rouen trial. William Manchon, priest and notary of the local ecclesiastical court, was constrained by English orders to act as recorder. When Bishop Cauchon bade him choose a collaborator, he suggested his friend William Colles, called Boisguillaume, another local priest and notary, who was duly appointed. Both testified at the rehabilitation, and though Manchon's testimony has in certain details been questioned, the probity and competence of both men are above suspicion. They entered into their functions on February 13, 1431, and were present at all the sessions during which Joan was questioned, though not at certain preliminary meetings of the court. The third *greffier*, Nicholas Taquel or Taquet, also a priest and notary, played a very minor role as recorder for the Vice-Inquisitor John Lemaître, Dominican friar, who, greatly against his inclination, was forced to join Cauchon as judge, and who began to function as such on March 13, after Joan had been questioned six times publicly and three times privately. Taquel stated at the rehabilitation that he had written nothing at the trial. However, he added his signature to those of Manchon and Boisguillaume at the end of the official account of the Rouen proceedings in testimony of having collated this with the original register.

How was this original register composed? At each session of the interrogatories, Manchon and Boisguillaume took notes, which were afterwards discussed, abridged, and put into final form at afternoon meetings in Bishop Cauchon's apartments, in the presence of several "assessors."[1] These meetings were often stormy, since, besides the official notaries, there were English clerks hidden in

---

[1] Men who "sit by" to assist or advise the judge.

the room where Joan was being questioned, who reported her answers in a highly arbitrary way; but efforts to make the notaries accept the versions of these irresponsible individuals were stubbornly resisted.

From the notes of Boisguillaume and 'his own, Manchon compiled a *minuta in Gallico* or "French minute" (though it included Latin accounts of several deliberations). This precious minute in Manchon's handwriting was given by him to the judges at the rehabilitation and afterwards disappeared, but has been shown by Jules Quicherat[2] to have survived, though only in part, in the so-called d'Urfé Manuscript. It must have been copied into the original register of the Rouen trial, which has been lost.

Some years after Joan's execution, probably not before 1435, Thomas de Courcelles, master of arts, bachelor of theology, distinguished Latinist and a leader among the assessors at Rouen, was ordered by Cauchon to prepare an official account of the proceedings, that they might be vindicated in the eyes of Christendom. Courcelles seems to have been more notable for brilliance than for frankness. Aeneas Sylvius Piccolomini, afterwards Pope Pius II, praised his modesty at the Council of Basle, saying that he "always looked at the ground and seemed a man who wished to hide himself." He certainly was such a man in more senses than one. For a comparison of the French minute of Joan's trial with the final Latin version shows that Courcelles omitted, in the latter, accounts of certain deliberations in which he had taken part, including one in which he had voted to submit Joan to torture. He feared, it is reasonable to infer, that the record of these matters might some day prove personally embarrassing. Ques-

---

[2] For authors and titles of works referred to in this book see the bibliographical note, pages 93 and 94.

tioned at the rehabilitation, moreover, he suffered from numerous lapses of memory, minimized his activities at the trial, and expressly denied having deliberated concerning the proposed torture of Joan.

It was this self-effacing gentleman, then, who, assisted by Manchon, drew up the official account of the proceedings at Rouen. He did so by translating the interrogatories into Latin, and by arranging all the accounts of the deliberations, with other relevant documents, in an orderly manner. Five copies of this account were made, three of them by Manchon himself. One of the five was ceremonially mutilated at the close of the rehabilitation process; another, probably sent to Rome, is lost. The remaining three, however, are still preserved in Paris. They are attested on each leaf by Boisguillaume, and at the end (but before certain appendices) by all three notaries. Each bears the seals of Bishop Cauchon and of the Vice-Inquisitor Lemaître. There are several later copies of these authentic manuscripts.

Original redactions of the documents compiled at the rehabilitation have also survived. They include, besides a large number of summations, patents, and so forth, of merely technical interest, two essential elements. In the first place, there are the sworn depositions of one hundred and seventeen persons (one hundred-twenty, if the witnesses heard only at the royal investigation be counted), nearly all of whom had known Joan personally. Abundant testimony was thus given as to her childhood, the early part of her military career, and the conduct of the Rouen trial, though there is, perhaps for political reasons, almost complete silence concerning the months preceding her capture at Compiègne, and those that passed during her captivity until the trial began at Rouen.

The second essential element in the rehabilitation documents consists of the briefs or memoirs prepared by theologians and canonists. They deal exhaustively with the legality of the trial and the charges against Joan, but add no additional data to our knowledge of her life, since they are based on the records of the trial and the depositions just mentioned. For this reason they have been much neglected by historians, and Quicherat did not think them sufficiently interesting to be edited *in toto*. They are, nevertheless, of prime importance for the subject of this book. Certain other similar memoirs, though prepared for the occasion, were not included in the dossier.

The notaries for the rehabilitation process were Denis Le Comte and Francis Ferrebouc. Since, however, depositions of witnesses were taken at Domrémy, Vaucouleurs, Orleans, and elsewhere, as well as at Paris and Rouen, the notaries had to delegate a considerable portion of their duties to local substitutes. Le Comte and Ferrebouc are accused by Quicherat of great slovenliness in regard to names, dates, and so forth, and are said to have made the usual attestations "with their eyes closed." There is something in the charge, no doubt, but it must be remembered that Quicherat, for reasons to be discussed later, developed an extremely hypercritical attitude toward the rehabilitation process as a whole. At any rate, its notaries showed less competence than did Manchon and Bois-guillaume, and there was no guiding hand in charge of their compilation comparable to that of Master de Courcelles.

A portion of a preliminary redaction of the enormous rehabilitation dossier has survived in the d'Urfé Manuscript, which also contains, as will be remembered, part of the "French minute" made at Rouen. The final redaction was made in triplicate, with considerable modifications in plan and style, and a long preface by the notaries.

The copy on which Quicherat based his text includes, besides the depositions of witnesses, nine theological memoirs, drawn up for the tribunal at the rehabilitation, or accepted by it. The most important is the masterly summing up called the *Recollectio,* by the Inquisitor John Bréhal, who, together with the archbishop of Rheims, the Bishop of Paris, and the Bishop of Coutances, made up the tribunal, which was constituted in 1455. The *Recollectio* utilizes not only the other theological memoirs, but also the evidence of witnesses. (For excerpts from Bréhal's *Recollectio* see Appendix A.)

Another copy of the dossier, presented to the library of Notre Dame of Paris by Bishop Chartier, one of the judges, includes one memoir only, that of the famous Chancellor Gerson, written during Joan's lifetime. In Quicherat's day the third original transcript was supposed to have been lost, but it has been conclusively identified by Pierre Champion among the manuscripts of the British Museum. It includes five memoirs besides the *Recollectio*.

Thus all three official copies of the rehabilitation dossier are now known to have survived. There are many derivative copies, one of which has a special interest because of a colored miniature of the Maid, not drawn from life of course, but noteworthy as among the earliest attempts to portray her. (See frontispiece.)

How far is it possible to determine the trustworthiness of these two great records, that of the condemnation and that of the rehabilitation?

As to the former, it must be remembered that the reports of the interrogatories were necessarily abridged. There was no system of stenographic reporting, at least none comparable to modern ones. The sessions of questioning normally lasted several hours, but the reading aloud of the longest report of a day's session would take

much less than half an hour. Joan's first historian, moreover, the man at whose command the account of her trial
was put into final form was, though ostensibly her impartial judge, in reality her mortal enemy: Peter Cauchon,
Bishop of Beauvais. And Courcelles, whose skill is chiefly
responsible for the actual drawing up of the record, was
Cauchon's compliant creature. This does not mean that
extensive falsifications were practised; the notaries
showed considerable courage in assuring the accuracy of
the record; and Cauchon himself was too clever not to
desire every appearance of truth and legality in the account which he prepared for the Pope, the Emperor, and
the King of England. It means, however, in the first place,
that where Joan's replies are remarkable for vigorous
piety and sturdy common sense, as they so often are, we
can be sure of their authenticity, for Cauchon would
never have allowed inaccuracy in a direction favorable
to Joan. It means, moreover, that one may not unreason-
ably look for possible unfairness or even misrepresenta-
tion. Pierre Champion, second in importance to Quicherat
as editor of the Rouen records, maintains that careful
comparison of the French minute with the final Latin
version justifies this suspicion. "We can even see," he says,
"how those who put the French text into Latin have sometimes made it more specific, modified it, and even falsi-
fied it in a sense unfavorable to the accused."

The record may reasonably be suspected of such falsi-
fication chiefly in regard to two events of the trial,
namely, the "Abjuration" of May 24, 1431, and the so-
called Posthumous Information, which professes to describe an interview in Joan's prison, on the morning of
her execution, May 30, between Joan, her two judges
(Cauchon and the Vice-Inquisitor Lemaître), and several
assessors. These matters, which will be discussed in their

places, have been the subject of extensive controversy, involving especially the general character of the rehabilitation testimony, which has a good deal to say about them. This testimony was given in 1452, 1455, and 1456, except for that of a few witnesses, given at the royal investigation of 1450. In so far as it relates to the trial at Rouen, it came from men who, willingly or not, had played a part in the condemnation of Joan, and who now found themselves called upon to describe, before authorities of diametrically opposite temper, the roles they had played at Rouen. Naturally they did so, as far as possible, in a manner favorable to themselves. Courcelles, as we have seen, actually lied when he denied having voted to submit Joan to torture.

In such ways there was no doubt something less than complete frankness, and there may have been on the other hand, exaggeration in the statements regarding the violence and highhandedness of Bishop Cauchon, who was dead in 1456, as was the Vice-Inquisitor Lemaître. Yet the testimony was given under oath, and there is no evidence of coercion. Those who had nothing to say in regard to questions asked them, or professed to forget what had happened, could apparently take such stands with impunity. Nor was it any part of the court's function to punish those involved in the Rouen trial, beyond condemning their conduct, since the king had declared an amnesty toward all who had been living in Normandy during the English occupation. So that, while evidence given at the rehabilitation need not all be accepted as indisputably true, it deserves careful consideration and ought not to be lightly rejected. When it conflicts with the official record of the trial it has at least an equal claim to be believed. Unsupported statements as to its worthlessness, because of alleged political pressure, are particularly unconvincing when made by writers who accept as gospel truth every word of the Rouen records, so thoroughly dominated by Cauchon. It may be added that there is no biographer of Joan, however critical of the rehabilitation testimony, who does not draw freely from this indispensable source.

2

HISTORIANS AND DOCUMENTS

THE treatment which the two records, that of the trial and that of the rehabilitation, have received from historians is in many cases surprising. The conclusions which it reaches have been brilliantly summarized by Mr. Bernard Shaw, in the preface of his highly effective but quite unhistorical play, which has done much to popularize the view he adopts.

Joan, he tells us, was both heretic and saint, in fact, "one of the first Protestant martyrs." "Her notion of the Catholic Church was one in which the Pope was Pope Joan." She had a fair trial, and the decision was strictly according to law. Bishop Cauchon, though Mr. Shaw admits having flattered him in order to present "the innermost ascertainable truth of the situation," was guilty neither of bad faith nor of exceptional severity. The Church, however, for which Mr. Shaw has very real respect, was, he tells us, capable of the "magnificently Catholic gesture" of canonizing a Protestant saint, as "a person of heroic virtue whose private judgment is privileged." This is what, centuries after a rehabilitation which the play describes as full of perjury and corruption, the Church proceeded to do. So far Mr. Shaw.

If the Irish playwright were solely responsible for this thesis, it would be a matter of minor interest, for no well-informed person is likely to regard the play as a contribution to historical science. However, though Shaw, with his keen sense of dramatic effect, has deliberately simplified and exaggerated the "conflict" with which he deals, he did not have to invent the essentials. Similar interpretations of the voluminous evidence concerning Joan are found in the works of influential historians, whom Mr. Shaw shows every sign of having read.

Thus Michelet, though recognizing the illegality of Cauchon's refusal to allow Joan's appeal to the Pope — an appeal totally ignored by Mr. Shaw — considers that the vital question involved a struggle between "the visible Church and authority on the one hand, and, on the other, inspiration testifying to the invisible Church." Joan's Church, he tells us, "was visible only in her heart." "There God shone; how dim He was elsewhere!"

The same idea concerning Joan is expressed by Henri Martin. "It is the struggle," he writes, "of organized tradition, the external rule, constituted infallibility, against individual spontaneity, immediate inspiration, the interior voice."

Especially influential has been the short study of Joan's trial and condemnation made by Jules Quicherat in his *Aperçus nouveaux sur l'histoire de Jeanne d'Arc,* published in 1850.

During the preceding decade this brilliant young paleographer had given to the learned world the first complete, or almost complete, edition of the documents relevant to Joan's trial and rehabilitation, a work which has been of inestimable value to all subsequent historians of the Maid. When, however, the paleographer became a critic in his *Aperçus nouveaux,* his interpretation of the data he knew so well was in some respects highly debatable. He concluded that the trial was irreproachably legal in form, and that the documents recording it were completely trustworthy; he relied to a surprising extent

on the word of Cauchon, though he described the bishop
as "a passionate, guileful, and corrupt man"; and he cast
doubt on the testimony given at the rehabilitation by
stating that "the depositions of the witnesses which form
the principal part appear to have been subjected to
numerous excisions."

It is useful to consider the relationship of these statements to each other. They are agreed with, wholly or in
part, by many historians hostile or at least alien to the
Church. It is, I believe, from the mentality of such historians rather than from objective study of the evidence,
that their conclusions spring. For to historians of this
stamp it is, as it were, axiomatic, that the Church *must* be
the eternal enemy of any individual's claim to private inspiration, that she must attempt to crush it, and that the
recognition of such inspiration is a peculiar prerogative
of Protestantism and free thought. If this be true, it follows that Bishop Cauchon's tribunal was, from the
Church's point of view, after all, right, and that Joan was
really a heretic. Her trial, however horrible in its outcome,
was therefore — again from the Church's supposed viewpoint — just, and the verdict deserved. Consequently the
rehabilitation process, which culminated with the quash-
ing and annulling of the earlier verdict, was a striking
example of self-contradiction by the Church. Thereby, to
quote Quicherat, who is here less discriminating than Mr.
Shaw, "the infallible Church reduced to nothingness a
whole case directed and judged by the Church." Moreover, if the first verdict was "just," there was no need of
resorting to illegal procedure in order to arrive at it, nor
of distorting any facts in the official account of the trial.
The rehabilitation process, which accuses Cauchon of
doing both, thus becomes guilty, as Shaw says, of "calumny of the dead," and is presumably unreliable in other

ways. In any case, it was, so to speak, a thoroughly un-Catholic process, and must have been inspired by purely political motives.

Such is the relationship between the theses supported by the historians in question. Starting from the assumption that the first trial was a true and characteristic expression of medieval Catholicism, they tend to defend its legality, and, in a way that seems at first sight paradoxical, to whitewash one of the most unlovely bishops of all time. As a consequence they view with suspicion the process of rehabilitation, incline to question the testimony given there, and regard themselves as freed from the onerous and uncongenial task of carefully studying the accompanying memoirs, and especially the *Recollectio* of Bréhal. I do not for a moment suggest that Quicherat or any other historian has deliberately set out to distort the evidence. But I believe that, under the more or less unconscious influence of a certain attitude toward the medieval Church, the evidence has often been dealt with in a very arbitrary way. An inspection of this evidence, conducted without the initial assumption of Joan's heresy, will, as I hope to show, reach very different conclusions.

3

DOMRÉMY TO POITIERS

JOAN OF ARC, called Jeannette in her childhood, was
born January 6, 1412, in Domrémy, on the confines of
Lorraine, the third child of Jacques d'Arc, a highly
respected peasant who was later *doyen* of his village, and
Isabelle (or Zabillet) Romée, his wife.

Her early childhood, concerning which her own statements at Rouen are confirmed and amply supplemented
by numerous deponents at the rehabilitation, was marked
by exceptional piety. Relatives, friends, and neighbors,
clerical and lay, including three godmothers (she had
several godparents of either sex, as was then the custom),
agreed, mostly from personal observation, that Joan's conduct as a child was always exemplary, that she knew her
prayers, was suitably instructed in the faith, knelt in the
fields when she heard the angelus bell, loved to go to
Mass and other services, often went to confession, and received Communion at Easter and other great feasts.
Later, during her military career, she received Communion almost weekly, which was at that time most un-
usual for a lay person, however devout.

Joan tells us at Rouen that she first saw her visions and
heard her voices when she was "about thirteen," but said
nothing about them to anyone, fearing parental opposition to the mission which the saints had laid upon her,
and also lest the Burgundians, who held territory near
Domrémy, might hear of her and try to prevent her going

to join the Dauphin. She could, of course, have safely spoken of her visions to her confessor, but her certainty of their divine origin no doubt made her regard this as unnecessary. She must, however, have spoken of her mission in a general way to her cousin's husband or "uncle," Durand Laxart, when she persuaded him to take her to Vaucouleurs in the spring of 1428; and her claim to be the divinely commissioned means of delivering France then became generally known. Yet, as far as the record shows, she did not describe her visions of St. Michael, St. Margaret, and St. Catherine in detail until her questioners at Rouen wrung the facts from her.

Captain Robert de Baudricourt, in command at Vaucouleurs, rebuffed Joan when she pleaded to be sent to the Dauphin, and she returned home. Later in the same year, the menace of a raid by Burgundian troops caused her family, together with other villagers of Domrémy, to flee for a short time to the near-by town of Neufchâteau.

After further urging by her voices, Joan returned to Vaucouleurs with Laxart early in 1429; whence, owing to the good offices of John de Metz (afterwards her treasurer) and Bertrand de Poulengy, she started for Chinon late in February, dressed as a soldier, and accompanied by the two gentlemen mentioned, and by four followers. The little cavalcade, avoiding the menace of hostile soldiery, reached its destination on March 6.

The Dauphin at first hesitated to see Joan. She told the officials who received her that God had sent her to deliver Orleans and to have the Dauphin crowned at Rheims. When Charles at length ordered her brought into his presence, "he retired apart," says an eyewitness, "behind the others; she recognized him none the less, and made obeisance to him." (The chronicler John Chartier, accurately or not, describes this famous recognition with details that make it more remarkable.) Joan told the Dauphin things known only to God and to himself. Either before or after her first interview with Charles (the testimony on this point is conflicting), he caused her to be questioned by several bishops and theologians, who reported favorably. These interrogatories at Chinon mark Joan's first encounter with ecclesiastical authority in regard to her mission.

The Dauphin then decided that a more thorough examination of Joan should be held by the clerics of the University of Poitiers, where the royal council was also about to convene. Thither Joan accompanied the court, later in the month of March.

The sessions at Poitiers lasted three weeks. An official record was kept, or at least Joan thought it had been, since she appealed several times at Rouen to the "book" or "register" of Poitiers; but this important document was not produced at the rehabilitation. It seems to have been already lost at that time, and has not been discovered since. We depend, therefore, on other sources for our knowledge of the proceedings. Several chroniclers give the opinion which the doctors rendered to the Dauphin after their investigations of Joan, and several witnesses at the rehabilitation supply further information.

By far the most important deposition, and the only one by a member of the examining board, is that of Brother Séguin de Séguin, professor of theology at Poitiers. After mentioning other theologians on the board, Brother Séguin tells us that Joan was questioned at the house of John Rabateau, where she lodged. Master Rabateau's wife (says another witness) was greatly edified by Joan's frequent and prolonged devotions. When a theologian asked Joan, the friar reports, why God needed soldiers to deliver France, she answered: "In God's name, the men-at-arms will fight, and God will give the victory!" Friar Séguin, who came from Limoges, asked Joan what "idiom" her voices spoke. "A better one than yours," she replied. Asked for a sign, Joan demanded that she be given troops and sent to Orleans.

"And she foretold," Séguin continues, "to me and to all the rest of us who were there, that these four things would happen: that the siege of Orleans would be raised and the city delivered, the English destroyed, the King crowned at Rheims, Paris restored to its obedience, and the Duke of Orleans brought back from England. And indeed I myself have seen these four things accomplished.

"We reported all this to the royal council, and were of the opinion that, in view of the extreme necessity and the great peril in which the city lay, the king might use her help and send her to Orleans.

"Before this, we had investigated her life and her morals, and we had found that she was a good Christian, living as a Catholic should, never idle. That her life and habits might be better known, women had been placed with her whose duty it was to report to the council her actions and thoughts."

The investigation at Poitiers, though somewhat informal in its procedure, was none the less official, carefully and thoroughly conducted under the authority of Reginald of Chartres, Archbishop of Rheims. The opinion which the board reported — though necessarily contingent upon the fulfillment of the chief "sign" which Joan had offered, namely, the deliverance of Orleans — was emphatic. "The king," its final sentences declare, "since he has made probation of the said Maid as far as possible, and finds no evil in her, and considering her answer, which is to show a divine sign before Orleans; in view of her constancy and her perseverance in her proposal, and her urgent requests to go to Orleans to show there a sign of divine help, should not prevent her from going to Orleans with his men-at-arms, but, with hope in God, should cause her to be honorably taken there. For to doubt her or dismiss her without any appearance of evil, would be to oppose the Holy Ghost and to render one's self unworthy of God's help, as said Gamaliel, in a council of the Jews, in regard to the Apostles."

Such a decision obviously acquired greater force when the deliverance of Orleans was actually accomplished. That Joan, in spite of replies so sturdily independent as to seem lacking in respect, should have gained it from a formidable group of churchmen who had no predisposition in her favor, is a fact of great importance. Joan realized its bearing on the legality of the Rouen trial as is shown by her own words. We shall see, in our study of Master Bréhal's *Recollectio,* that she was not mistaken.

4

THE ASCENT TO RHEIMS

ABOUT the twentieth of April, Joan, now accepted by the Dauphin, was sent to Tours. Here she was equipped with armor, including the sword which was found, as her voices told her it would be, buried near the altar of the Church of St. Catherine at Fierbois. The famous standard, representing our Lord enthroned between angels, with the inscription *Jesus Maria,* was prepared for her. Her military household was formed. It included her brothers John and Peter, John de Metz, and Bertrand de Poulengy (the two soldiers who had accompanied her from Vaucouleurs); and Brother John Pasquerel, an Augustinian friar who had met her mother at Le Puy, as her chaplain and confessor.

In a few days Joan moved on to Blois, where an army gathered, variously estimated at from 3000 to 12,000 men. They marched on Orleans, led by the clergy singing the *Veni Creator,* and arrived on April 28 opposite the city, on the southern bank of the Loire. Here Joan was joined by a man who was to be closely associated with her military career, Dunois, the Bastard of Orleans, commander of the garrison. For the "siege" of Orleans, begun in the previous October, was not such as to prevent frequent French excursions, or the entrance of provisions in considerable quantities. It consisted rather in sporadic attacks by the English, made from the numerous forts which they had built for the purpose, mostly west of the

19

city, and southwards, across the Loire. Joan was able to cross the river with a force of two hundred lances, and, on the evening of April 29, to enter Orleans by the eastern gate, amid great popular acclaim. Next day she sent the first of several similar letters (it seems to have been dictated at Poitiers) summoning the English to surrender to the envoy of God.

After a pause in hostilities, there followed a complicated series of attacks on the forts, culminating in that against the Tourelles, stone towers built on an arch of the broken bridge over the Loire. Here, on May 7, when an all-day battle had failed to bring victory to the French, Joan, though wounded in the shoulder by an arrow, rallied her troops after the recall had actually been sounded. Their furious assault from the south, aided by troops from the city who had succeeded in temporarily spanning the broken arches of the bridge, carried the Tourelles and decided the struggle for Orleans. Next day the English retired, after the two armies had for a time confronted each other without fighting. Rapturous celebrations followed in the city, and the religious ceremonies accompanying them have been annually observed until our own times, except for an interruption of some years during the French Revolution.

Joan lost no time in rejoining the Dauphin at Tours. News of her victory was officially sent to the still loyal cities, and spread rapidly beyond the confines of France. The blow to British prestige, and the corresponding rise of French morale, especially in territory held by the English and Burgundians, was considerable. The legend of a conqueror's invincibility had been shattered.

At this time Joan received encouragement from two important churchmen: James Gelu, Archbishop of Embrun, and the aged John Gerson, one time Chancellor of the

University of Paris, both of whom wrote treatises warmly supporting the Maid. The former came to her defense once more during the time of her captivity, by rebuking the king for his failure to ransom her. The latter's treatise was incorporated, some twenty-five years later, into the dossier of her rehabilitation, thus receiving the sanction of the tribunal which, under papal authority, conducted that affair.

Joan was now eager for action. She longed to see the Dauphin crowned at Rheims with the least possible delay, but Charles procrastinated as usual, preferring to spend precious hours in endless discussions, which included a plan for the invasion of Normandy. One day, at Loches, Joan entered the room where the Dauphin was in council, clasped his knees as a suppliant, and exclaimed: "Noble Dauphin, hold no more wordy councils, but come with all speed to Rheims and be worthily crowned!"

After a wasted month it was decided that she should accompany an expedition to deliver the cities of the Loire valley before attempting the march to Rheims. The force was commanded by a prince of the blood royal, John, Duke of Alençon, who had been Joan's friend since her first arrival at Chinon.

The question of Joan's military rank may be briefly treated here. In one of her letters to the English she had spoken of herself as "chef de guerre," but unless she was referring to her divine commission, the term seems to be roughly equivalent to "captain." So far, at any rate, she had *official* command only over the handful of men who formed her "military household," though others could and did rally to her standard in battle. By November, 1429, however, she was referred to in official documents, together with d'Albret, Lieutenant General for Berri, as one of the two commanders of the French forces.

Passing through Orleans on June 9, the army marched on to Jargeau, a few miles eastward, just as Sir John Fastolf was leaving Paris with English reinforcements. Largely owing to Joan's insistence on an immediate assault, after the English had refused terms of surrender, the town yielded in a few days, and the Earl of Suffolk was taken prisoner. After a return to Orleans, the bridgehead at Meun, to the west, was taken, and Beaugency, further down the Loire, surrendered soon after. Large English reinforcements arrived, under Fastolf and Talbot, and fell back on Meun, whence they began a retreat toward Paris.

The French, now numerically superior, followed through woods which concealed the enemy troops; but when English shouts at a fleeing stag revealed their whereabouts near Patay, the French attacked unexpectedly, and a great victory was won. Several thousand men were killed or captured. Joan, greatly to her displeasure, was in the rear. Her page told afterwards of her comforting a dying Englishman.

She returned once more to Orleans after this "week of victories." The Dauphin was away visiting his favorite La Trémoïlle at Sully, but joined Joan near by on June 22. There were further exasperating councils and delays, till Joan was allowed to begin the march northeastwards. She set out from Gien, on the Loire, June 27, followed next day by the Dauphin.

Several important towns lay in their path. Auxerre, Burgundian in sympathy, seems to have escaped attack by bribing La Trémoïlle. When the army reached Troyes, the party bent on appeasing Burgundy, led by La Trémoïlle and the Archbishop of Rheims, were all for retreating; but the town, where an eccentric popular preacher had come over to Joan's side, surrendered after seeing the energetic preparations for an attack on which she had insisted. Châlons was also entered without a struggle. On July 16, the Dauphin was willingly received at Rheims.

Next day he was crowned in the Cathedral, with a crown of no special value from the treasury, since he had apparently neglected to bring his own. The Duke of Burgundy was conspicuous by his absence from his cere-monial functions, but all else was carried out according to the ancient ritual. Archbishop Reginald administered the oath, oil from the "holy phial" of St. Remigius was poured on Charles's head, and the people shouted "Noël!" Joan stood near by with her banner. As she said at her trial: "It had been in the struggle, and it was most fitting that it should be in the glory." After the ceremony, she exclaimed amid her tears: "Gentle King, now is ac-complished the will of God, who decreed that I should raise the siege of Orleans and bring you to this city of Rheims to receive your solemn sacring, thereby showing that you are the true King, and that France should be yours."

"And right great pity came upon all who saw her," we are told, "and many wept."

5

THE LONG DESCENT

ON that same day an offer of peace arrived from the Duke of Burgundy. Joan, though convinced that no peace could be made with the English while they remained in France, was herself desirous of making peace with the Duke, but the "long, good, and assured peace" which she hoped for was not at all the sort which Philip was prepared to offer. As a matter of fact, while the King was wasting four days in negotiations at Rheims, Cardinal Beaufort, great-uncle of the boy King Henry VI, was bringing 3500 men (mustered ostensibly to fight the Hussites in Bohemia) from Calais to Paris, and Burgundy was sending recruits to the English forces.

On July 21, the French army left Rheims, and, after entering Soissons, crossed the Marne at Château-Thierry, then, to Joan's disgust, headed south toward Charles's beloved Loire on August 1. She was glad when, some days later, this retreat was cut off by English forces, but she was still depressed. Riding along one day, she was asked by the Archbishop of Rheims where she expected to die. "Where God pleases," she replied, "and would it were God's pleasure that I might now lay down my arms and go back to serve my father and mother." Her *via dolorosa* had begun, and the glory of Rheims was never to return.

At this time the Duke of Bedford sent a highly insulting letter to Charles, challenging him to fight in open field. Joan expected such a battle near Senlis on August 15, but the English refused to sally forth from their palisaded camp, and an assault on this was wisely declined by the French. Only a few skirmishes took place.

Compiègne, Senlis, and Beauvais had surrendered to the King and the Maid by August 22. From the last named town, his episcopal see, fled Peter Cauchon, Joan's archenemy, who was to try and condemn her at Rouen.

At Compiègne, Charles again became involved in negotiations with Burgundy, while Joan sorrowed. She left the King there, occupied St. Denis, and repeatedly reconnoitered the walls of Paris with d'Alençon.

On August 28, the King concluded with Philip of Burgundy an amazing armistice, which was to last till Christmas, and was afterwards prolonged till the spring. It provided that Charles might attack Paris, but that Burgundy might help the English to defend it! The town of Compiègne was to be loaned to Philip, but he refused to accept this arrangement.

Joan's attack on Paris, September 8, concerning which the accounts do not agree, seems to have been, in the purpose of the other French leaders, a mere skirmish or display, designed to help a tumult and possible revolt by French sympathizers in the city. Joan, however, intended to make of it a much more serious engagement. In any case, it failed. The Porte Saint Honoré was attacked with initial success, but, after sunset, Joan was wounded in the thigh by an arrow. She continued to encourage her men, but was at length carried out of fire, protesting. Early next morning, at her camp near the city, she was urging d'Alençon to sound the trumpets for an advance, when the King's orders arrived, bidding her return at once to Saint Denis. Charles had even destroyed a bridge over the Seine, thus preventing another move against Paris next day.

After a hasty retreat southwards, Charles and his army were back at Gien, on the Loire, by September 21. The forces were there disbanded, though Joan remained, in harrowing idleness, with the King.

For a time she could do nothing but follow in the train of the Court. The King was constantly moving from place to place, but the Queen settled for some time at Bourges, and there Joan lodged for three weeks with a lady who afterward praised her innocence and her kindness to the poor.

In the fall of 1429, Charles's advisers decided to anticipate probable Burgundian plans by seizing the towns of St. Pierre le Moustier and La Charité, not far east of Bourges. The former was brilliantly taken by a force under the Maid and d'Albret, but from the latter, the besiegers were forced to withdraw, owing to the lateness of the season and to lack of supplies, which only the faithful city of Orleans was able to furnish.

Winter wore on, while the King lavished money on La Trémoïlle. The ill-kept truce with Burgundy, the chief effect of which seems to have been to prevent a wholehearted attack on Paris from being attempted, expired in the spring. Joan wrote encouragingly to the people of Rheims, and her confessor, Brother John Pasquerel, sent stern admonishments on her behalf to the Bohemian heretics.

Philip of Burgundy himself wrote a long paper of advice to the English Council at this time. It sets forth plans for the spring campaign, and testifies to the enormous change in the military situation which Joan had brought about. With friend and foe her reputation was indeed still great, yet she no longer received effective backing from her King, who was only just beginning to realize that his hopes of peace by means of appeasing Burgundy were illusory — a fact which Joan had long since known.

Late in March, 1430, the Maid, unable to refrain any longer from attempts at military action in the region near Paris, left Sully (La Trémoïlle's seat) with "two or three lances," and joined the small forces of certain captains, including a Scot and a Lombard, whom she encountered.

In Easter week (April 17–23) at Melun, which ejected its Burgundian garrison to receive her, Joan's voices warned her that she would be captured before Mid-summer Day. Yet, in spite of this terrible foreknowledge she rode on. At Lagny, after reinforcements had arrived, she won a minor victory over a band allied with the English. Then she moved on to Senlis with a larger force.

The little King Henry VI had landed at Calais on April 23, and his Council hoped that he, too, might be crowned at Rheims. The capture of Compiègne now became of vital importance for the relief of Paris in Anglo-Burgundian plans. After a series of maneuvers, Joan, hearing at Crépy that Compiègne was menaced by large enemy forces, hurried thither with three or four hundred men, and arrived in the dawn of May 24. That afternoon she led a sudden sortie across the Aisne, and routed the small Burgundian force there encamped. Her withdrawal into the town would have been assured, had not several Burgundian officers chanced to come from Clairvoix near by, observed the affray, and sent for strong reinforcements. Joan for a time kept them at bay, but most of her troops had fled by boats and bridge. She was finally dragged from her horse in the swampy meadow by an archer of the Bastard of Wandomme, vassal of the Burgundian John of Luxemburg. John d'Aulon, her devoted companion since Chinon, was captured with her.

There was great jubilation in the enemy camp. The Duke of Burgundy came to gaze at the witch. The Vicar-

General of the Inquisition wrote from Paris, on the day after he had received the news, to Philip, demanding that Joan be handed over to be tried for heresy. The University of Paris wrote repeatedly to Philip and to John of Luxemburg, urgently making the same demand. The relative portions of theological zeal and political interest in the attitude of the *Alma Mater* have been much discussed. Both were present; the former was that of a body which regarded itself as the supreme theological authority in Christendom, the latter that of men who found their positions and emoluments menaced by upheavals in the *status quo*, which therefore *must* come from the devil.

On July 14, Bishop Pierre Cauchon, chosen to represent the English government in the affair, and handsomely paid by them till the end of the trial, delivered in person to Philip and John his letter offering ten thousand francs — a royal ransom, as he said — for Joan, and claiming the right to try her, "as she had been taken in his diocese."

In the meantime, Joan, after a few days at Clairvoix, was taken to the castle of Beaulieu for a fortnight, thence forty miles north to John's castle of Beaurevoir. Here she stayed for four months, till the end of September, kindly treated by three other Joans, aunt, wife, and daughter of the Luxemburger. The oldest of the ladies begged her nephew not to deliver the Maid to the English. Joan would never promise not to try to escape. At Beaurevoir she made the attempt, in spite of her voices' opposition, by leaping from a sixty-foot tower, and was grievously, though temporarily, lamed. The court at Rouen made much of this, professing to regard it as an attempt at suicide. They could blame her for disobeying her voices when it suited them!

Negotiations between Cauchon and Burgundy dragged

on through September. Joan was moved to Arras, in Burgundian territory. In November the money had been raised and the horrible deal put through. The Maid was in English hands.

The University wrote again, this time to Cauchon, urging speed in bringing Joan to Paris, to be tried by them. They wrote a letter of similar tenor to Henry VI. On December 16 the boy was crowned King of France in Notre Dame of Paris, Rheims being inaccessible, by his great-uncle Cardinal Beaufort. Before the end of the year he had settled in Rouen.

It was probably shortly before that Joan had been brought thither, and lodged in the castle of Philip Augustus. She was no longer relatively free, but "in a dark cell, fettered and in irons."

The various competitors for the honor of doing the Maid to death reached an agreement: Cauchon was to try her at Rouen, for which the subservient chapter, the see being vacant, granted him such rights as they had; the Inquisition was to be represented as cojudge; the University was to assume a sort of general moral responsibility; those who spoke for Henry VI, while authorizing Cauchon to conduct the trial in a rescript dated January 3, 1431, reserved the right to take Joan back "if she were not convicted in any matter touching the faith" — a quite unnecessary precaution. In short, the stage was set.

What had Joan's party been doing to save her during all these months? The University had written to Burgundy of its anxiety lest this woman should be delivered out of his hands "by the guile and seduction of the infernal enemy, and by the malice and subtlety of evil persons" — said to be devoting all their energies to rescuing Joan. There was little ground for worry!

The Archbishop of Rheims, whom the Maid had restored to his see, complained to his spiritual subjects on the day after Joan's capture, that she "would not take advice, but did as she chose." He had actually espoused the cause of a new prophet, a shepherd boy who claimed that he, too, had been sent by God to deliver France.

The Venetian chronicler Morosini reported, on returning home from Bruges in December, 1430, rumors current in the Flemish city that Charles had written Burgundy on no account to deliver Joan to the English, under pain of reprisals against Burgundian captives. There is no confirming evidence of this.

Alone among prominent Frenchmen, as far as we know, James Gelu, Archbishop of Embrun, solemnly warned the King against the disgraceful ingratitude of failing to ransom the Maid.

6

TRIAL AND DEATH

THE trial of Joan of Arc at Rouen consisted, strictly speaking, of two trials: the *Causa Lapsus,* or investigation of the alleged crime, which began January 9, 1431, and ended with the so-called abjuration on May 24; and the much shorter *Causa Relapsus,* lasting from May 28 till May 31, which had merely to ascertain that the accused had violated, by word and deed, the engagements she was supposed to have assumed at the abjuration, and then to hand her over to the secular power for execution.

The *Causa Lapsus* was, moreover, itself divided into two parts. First came the *Processus ex Officio,* a preparatory procedure conducted by Bishop Cauchon, with the reluctant and purely formal assistance, from March 13 to 26, of the Vice-Inquisitor for the Rouen archdiocese, Brother John Lemaître. In this process a *prima facie* case against the accused was established, based on information collected for the purpose, and on her replies to questions asked her. Six interrogatory sessions were held in public, after which Cauchon decided to hold them in the presence of one or both judges and a few assessors only. There were nine such private sessions.

The second process, called the *Processus Ordinarius,* was in charge of the Promoter or Prosecutor d'Estivet, and lasted from March 27 to May 24. In this process charges against Joan were formulated in seventy articles, and read to the accused, who was "interpellated" concerning them. These articles were then boiled down to twelve by the assessor Nicholas Midi, discussed, condemned by numerous assessors, and submitted to the Paris faculties of Theology and of Canon Law, as also to certain eminent theologians in Normandy.

In the articles, Joan is never named, but is simply "a woman," while Charles VII is "a certain secular prince" or "her prince." The contending parties in the war are referred to once or twice, but no place is mentioned except, curiously enough, Compiègne. The only persons named are the saints. So that the general effect is almost that of a hypothetical "casus." Joan's assertions are summarized so as to make them appear in the most unfavorable light possible; her subsequent explanations and denials, often luminous in their piety and sound common sense, are ignored. The articles are far from succinct, for there is much overlapping, including repeated stress on Joan's conviction that her voices brought revelations from God, to be believed with the certainty of faith.

The substances of the articles is as follows:

I. The woman claims to have had, often under circumstances savoring of superstition, corporal visions of saints, who imposed on her a mission to a prince, that he might regain his kingdom. She says she is God's envoy and will bow to no man's judgment. (Besides matter repeated in the following articles.)

II. She convinced her prince by showing, as a sign, an angel bringing him a crown. (See Chapter 15.)

III. She is certain with the certainty of faith that it is St. Michael, St. Margaret, and St. Catherine who appear to her.

IV. She prophesies from her revelations that she will be delivered and that she will lead the French to military exploits of unexampled greatness; and states that she foretold where a hidden sword would be found.

V. By God's command, she says, she wears men's clothing, and nothing short of His command will make her abandon it.

VI. She has used the names of Jesus and Mary, and a cross, on her letters.

VII. Urged by her visions, she went at seventeen, against her parents' will, to find a knight, who took her to her prince, to whom she promised victory if he accepted her.

VIII. Preferring death to captivity, she leaped from a high tower, against her saints' advice. She admits that she thus sinned gravely but claims to have been forgiven by confession.

IX. She is certain of salvation if she preserves her virginity.

X. She knows from her saints, who speak to her in French, since they are not of the English party, that God loves certain persons more than she does. She has ceased to love the Burgundians, since her saints are on the other side.

XI. She has bowed down to her saints, touched them, and embraced them. She has never consulted a priest in the matter; and professes that she would have been well able to detect an evil spirit.

XII. Though frequently admonished, she refuses to submit her claims to the Church militant, especially in matters of faith.

The University lost no time in returning these articles with various condemnatory judgments by the faculties. These having been officially reported by Cauchon to the assessors, all present concurred in the Paris decisions, and concluded that a verdict should be delivered. The abjuration, which will be discussed later, took place during the reading of the sentence on May 24.

The important role of the three *greffiers* or recorders has been dealt with in Chapter 1.

The "assessors," whose function was purely consultative, consisted of more than sixty theologians and canonists, led by six especially famous ones from Paris, who were, incidentally, well paid by the English for their pains. Other assessors included twenty-one canons of the Rouen chapter (nine more took no part, and may have declined too), ten abbots or priors from the religious houses of Normandy, and a crowd of younger doctors, licentiates, and bachelors. The number present at public sessions, or taking part in deliberations, varied considerably. Less than half were much more active than the rest.

Was pressure brought to bear on them? In the vast majority of cases this was certainly unnecessary, for caution counseled silence where agreement was less than complete. Yet Cauchon was bent on Joan's destruction at all costs, and perfectly capable of resorting to threats, imprisonment, and so forth, in cases when it might be necessary to preserve the legal façade of his *"beau procès."* Several witnesses at the rehabilitation say that he did, with circumstantial details. Some historians hold that their testimony is exaggerated. It is hardly reasonable, however, to doubt the statement of Nicholas de Houppeville, summoned as an assessor, that he was imprisoned by Cauchon for criticizing the trial. It also seems probable that a certain John Lohier suffered because of his critical attitude.

Certain Norman bishops acted as consultors without taking part in the trial. Their lordships of Lisieux and Coustances concurred emphatically in the condemnation, but the aged and saintly Bishop of Avranches, according to Isambard de la Pierre, an assessor, refused to take part, saying that the matter was one for the Pope and the General Council. He was threatened by the prosecutor. The three remaining bishops were absent from their sees, one of them with Charles VII.

A brief mention of the state of the contemporary Church should help toward a better understanding of the trial. From 1378 to 1417 there had been two and then three rival claimants for the papal throne. The election of Martin V in the latter year, when Joan was five years old, left the need for reform unremedied and failed to reconcile those rival theories of Church government, monarchial and conciliar, which were struggling for the control of Christendom.

Martin died in February, 1431, soon after the Maid's trial began. Eugene IV, his successor, whatever rumors he may have heard of Joan, was at no time officially notified of her trial, though she appealed to him, as we shall see. The effect of action by Rome, had such been attempted, is in any case highly doubtful. For the University of Paris was the very spearhead of the party which held the superiority of a General Council to the Pope. It is not surprising, therefore, to find several of the Paris theologians hurrying from Rouen to the Council of Basle, which had begun its long and tumultuous activity, legally at least, during Joan's trial, though it did not really commence to function till the following December. Courcelles, afterward editor of Cauchon's official account of the Rouen proceedings, was particularly prominent at Basle, following the Council into its schism by separating itself from Eugene IV, whom it "deposed," and supporting for a time the anti-Pope Felix V.

Yet it is quite erroneous to regard opposition to full papal supremacy as a special tendency of Joan's enemies, as some have argued. Rather was it the doctrine of the whole "Gallican" Church, led by the University of Paris. It was shared by the prelates of Joan's party, notably Gelu and Gerson, and thoroughly supported by Charles VII. It lasted for centuries after English domination was a thing of the past.

One notes with interest that some of the assessors who had been most anxious to serve English interests at Rouen by their hostility to Joan, for instance, Courcelles and Midi, found no difficulty in reconciling themselves to Charles VII when that became necessary. Midi welcomed the King in 1436, with a long discourse on behalf of the University, while Courcelles preached his funeral sermon in 1461.

7

ABJURATION AND RELAPSE

LEAVING a systematic criticism of the trial till that can be undertaken in connection with the study of Bréhal's *Recollectio* (see p. 6), let us now consider in some detail two closely related episodes, concerning which the character of the record raises grave doubts as to accuracy, or, at the very least, completeness.

On the morning of May 24, 1431, according to the official account, a general public assembly was held in the cemetery of Saint Ouen at Rouen. It included, besides the two judges, Henry, Cardinal of Winchester, great-uncle of the boy king, Henry VI. It is the only time this immensely powerful prelate is mentioned as having been present at the proceedings of the trial, though he was certainly an important factor behind the scenes. There were also present three bishops, ten abbots or priors, twenty-seven theologians and canonists who are mentioned by name, many other assessors, and a great crowd of people. After Joan had been led to a scaffold in front of this formidable company, a sermon was preached by Master William Érart on the text: "The branch cannot bear fruit of itself unless it abide in the vine." Needless to say, the preacher denounced the alleged heresies of the Maid, and ended by calling on her to abjure them. This she refused to do, declaring that she had previously answered the court in regard to submission to the Church, that her words and deeds came from God, and that she

appealed — as she had before — to God and to the Pope.
She was told that the Pope was too far away, that bishops
were competent judges in their dioceses, and that she
must recognize the Church's authority in the judgment
which had been passed against her. Bishop Cauchon then
began the reading of the sentence, but when, after a
lengthy preamble, he came to the mention of Joan's name,
she interrupted him. She would submit, she cried, to the
Church and to her judges. If her visions and revelations
were condemned by churchmen, she would no longer
believe in them or uphold them.

Another document was then immediately produced
and read to her in French. This was the formula of abjuration, summing up the charges already made against
her. Therein she acknowledged herself guilty of invent-
ing visions and revelations, of superstitious divinations,
of blasphemy against God and the saints, of transgressing
divine and ecclesiastical law, of wearing clothing abhor-
rent to her sex, of bearing arms, of cruelly desiring the
shedding of blood, of despising God and the sacraments,
of worshiping and invoking evil spirits, of schismatical
conduct, and of errors against the faith.

We are told that she repeated this formula as it was
read to her and signed it with her hand. Its length, in
modern printed editions, is from forty to fifty odd lines,
depending on the size of type — a fact, as we shall see, of
great importance.

Cauchon, the account continues, then read to her
another formula, which freed her from excommunication,
but condemned her to a penance of perpetual imprisonment. Later in the day, the Vice-Inquisitor and others
visited Joan in the prison to which she had been returned,
exhorting her to remain penitent, and to resume female
clothing. She did so, and her hair was shaved from her

head. (It had been hitherto worn in the manner of a military man of the period, which means, not down to the shoulders, as she is often portrayed, but long to a point just above the ears and there cut off, with the lower part of the head shaved in the rear.)

Light is thrown on this account by the record of a visit which the two judges, several assessors, and the notaries, paid to Joan in her prison, on May 28, four days after the abjuration. On this occasion Joan was found to have resumed male clothing, and made in substance the following statements: —

She had resumed male clothing of her own free will, not having understood that she had sworn not to do so; because being among men (the soldiers who guarded her) it was more proper that she should be dressed as a man; and because the promises made to her, namely, that she would be allowed to hear Mass and receive Communion and would be released from chains, had not been kept. If they were kept, and she were put *en prison gracieuse* (i.e., an ecclesiastical prison) with a woman for attendant, she would do what the Church willed. —

Her voices, which had bidden her answer the preacher boldly on the scaffold, had since reproached her with having betrayed them by making the abjuration to save her life, and with acknowledging things she had not done. She had not understood the formula of abjuration, nor intended to deny that St. Margaret and St. Catherine had appeared to her. She had never said or done anything against God and the faith, and had said at the time that she did not intend to revoke anything, except in so far as it pleased our Lord. She would damn herself if she denied that God had sent her.

She would resume female clothing if the judges willed, but would do nothing as to the rest.

A comparison between the French minute and the final Latin version of this interview reveals not only certain additions in the latter, but also certain omissions. One of these at least is of the utmost importance as an example of the "falsifications" to which Champion refers. The words of the French text are: "She said *that she said at the time* that she did not intend to revoke anything except in so far as it was pleasing to our Lord"; but the Latin omits the words italicized, reading: "She said that she did not intend to revoke anything," etc. Thus Thomas de Courcelles, by omitting a phrase in his Latin version, made Joan's repudiation of her "abjuration" seem an afterthought, and concealed the fact that *she had stated at the time* that whatever she agreed to, she agreed to only conditionally. Even the Latin version shows, however, that she abjured because of certain promises made to her, and that these promises had not been kept. Joan's resumption of male clothing, previous to May 28, and her reassertion of the supernatural character of her voices and visions, constituted her "relapse," so that the account of this interview is the first document in the second trial. Returning to the abjuration itself, we find that testimony concerning it, given at the rehabilitation (or, in a few cases, at the royal investigation which preceded it), though it varies in minor details, is on the whole consistent.

This testimony states that Joan had been advised of the approaching exhortation and urged to declare her submission to the Church when the sermon was made. According to the notary Manchon, Nicholas Loyseleur, canon of Rouen, unscrupulous and implacable throughout the trial in his enmity to Joan, had promised her that she would suffer no harm if she submitted, but would be put into the hands of the Church, and hence into an ecclesiastical prison. She had repeatedly asked for this,

and again demanded it, according to Manchon and the
Bailiff John Massieu, at the close of the proceedings on
May 24, at which time the demand was as usual peremp-
torily refused by Cauchon. As we have seen, she asked
once more for this *prison gracieuse* on May 28. The matter
is of no small importance. In a church prison she would
have had a female attendant, as she reminded the judges
on May 28, a reminder which, be it noted, is mentioned
in the French minute only, and suppressed in the Latin
version. Thus situated, she would have had no reason for
the resumption of male clothing, which had been obviously necessary during her career, and which gave her
some degree of protection against the brutality of her
guards in the military prison.

Now the wearing of male clothing was an important
charge against her, being represented as not only contrary to divine and human law, but actually, with fan-
tastic absurdity, as evidence of errors concerning the
faith; and her resumption of man's apparel, resorted to for
reasons to be later discussed, shortly after the abjuration,
constituted therefore an element of major importance in
her "relapse." If, however, the promise made to her had
been kept, this part of her "relapse" would never have
occurred.

Several witnesses tell us that Joan, during the sermon
in the cemetery, reproached the preacher when he attacked her king. When she was hesitating after being
bidden to abjure, a chaplain of the English Cardinal accused Cauchon of favoring Joan, and was rebuked by his
master, who of course knew better. The English soldiery,
encouraged by the presence of the executioner, had expected Joan to be put to death then and there. As it became evident that this was not to be, their anger grew
more and more vociferous. Stones were thrown. Insults

were heaped on Joan as she was led back to prison, says
one witness, and the greatest indignation against Cauchon
was expressed. Certain English nobles, says the same witness, were even reported to have menaced the bishop and
his consultors with their swords. "The king fares ill,"
cried a noble, "Joan is saved!" "Do not worry, my lord,"
one of the doctors replied, "we shall know how to get her
back."

By far the most important testimony, however, con-
cerns the actual moment of abjuration. It is clear that,
whatever Joan did, she did after considerable hesitation,
lured by Érart's promises of deliverance, terrified by his
threats of impending death if she remained obdurate, and
committing herself to the Church. As to the manner of
her signing, Massieu says that she made a cross, and it has
been argued, not very convincingly, that she intended this
as a sign of rejection. Haimon de Macy, a layman, says
she made, "in derision," something round, and that an
English clerk seized her hand and made her sign
"Jehanne." Manchon is sure that she was smiling. John
de Mailly, Bishop of Noyon, says many looked on the
abjuration as a joke, and agrees with William du Désert,
canon of Rouen, that an English doctor wanted the abjuration rejected because Joan was laughing. The self-
effacing Courcelles, characteristically, can remember
almost nothing. As to what she signed, the testimony is
so important that I quote from it verbatim, transposing it
from the record into direct discourse:

John Massieu: When he had finished his sermon, Master
Érart, holding in his hand a form of abjuration, said to
Joan: "Abjure and sign this form." Érart passed it to me
to read to Joan, which I did. I remember that in this
form it was stated that she would no longer bear arms or
wear male clothing or short hair, and much more that I

do not remember. This form contained about eight lines, no more. It is certainly not the same as the one whose text is contained in the official trial; the one which I read to Joan, and which Joan signed, was quite different.

William Delachambre (a doctor of medicine, forced by Cauchon to assist at the trial): I was present at the sermon of Master William Érart; without remembering what he said, I recall Joan's abjuration. She took a very long time to make it. Master William Érart made her decide to do it by telling her that if she did she would be delivered from prison. She abjured only on that condition, and then read a certain little form containing six or seven lines on a double sheet of paper. I was so near her that I could see with certainty the lines and their number.

John Monnet (a clerk to one of the Parisian theologians): The Bishop of Beauvais asked the English Cardinal what he should do in view of Joan's submission. The cardinal answered the bishop that he should admit Joan to penance. Then the bishop put aside the sentence which he had already read in part, and admitted Joan to penance. I saw the form of abjuration which was read at that moment. It was, I think, a little form of six or seven lines. I remember very well that Joan had said that she would trust the conscience of the judges as to whether she should abjure or not.

Nicholas Taquel (notary for the Vice-Inquisitor Lemaître): At the sermon made on the Place Saint Ouen, I was not on the platform with the other notaries, but I was near enough to have seen and heard everything. I remember well having seen a form of abjuration, written in the French language, read to Joan. John Massieu read it to her. Joan repeated it as Massieu read. It comprised about six lines of large writing, and began thus: "I, Joan," and so forth.

⇠ We thus have the testimony of four witnesses, all of whom were standing close by, and one of whom, Massieu, had himself read the form of abjuration to Joan, that the form was a very brief one, whereas the form included in the record, in which Joan states that she signed it with her name and mark, includes some forty lines of small print. ⇠

Quicherat, in his *Aperçus nouveaux*, does his best to minimize the importance of this fact, in keeping with his general tendency to defend the regularity and legality of the trial against contrary evidence given at the rehabilitation. He denies that Joan either repeated and signed a form different from that included in the record, or that she repeated one form and was made to sign another. Cauchon, in Quicherat's estimation, was too clever to have resorted to such gross trickery. Even if there were two documents, he concludes, the longer differed from the shorter only by the addition of legal and theological verbiage.

Few historians have followed Quicherat in his denial of a substitution of documents, but many, sharing his general tendency, have agreed that the difference between the two forms was not a substantial one.

⸢Now the denial of any substitution involves a wholly gratuitous rejection of the sworn testimony of four eye-witnesses, merely because of an *a priori* assumption as to what Cauchon, whom Quicherat himself describes as a "passionate, guileful, and corrupt man," would or would not have done; and the assumption — for it is an assumption — that the two forms differed only in the addition of technical phrases to the shorter one, is, to say the least, hazardous.⸥ It contradicts the explicit statement of Massieu, who had read the form to Joan, and who is certain that it was "quite different" from the one inserted in the

record. Even if the form Joan signed was merely expand-
ed for the record, the latter would still be guilty of mis-
representing the facts, for Joan is therein stated to have
repeated and signed *that* form. There is, moreover, an
enormous difference between repeating and signing a
long formula, admitting, with many expressions of repentance, a lengthy list of charges, and signing, in a bewildering atmosphere of disorder and confusion, a much
more summary one.

What did the shorter form contain? Massieu mentions
only promises not to wear male clothing or bear arms. No
doubt the form included also some general expression of
submission to the Church. Did it disavow Joan's inspiration, and if so, to what extent? We can never know posi-
tively, though her bitter self-reproaches, uttered in the
prison interview four days later, speak of "betrayal" of
her voices. For the evidence as a whole shows, not that
Joan had been in any real sense guilty, with full deliberation and consent, of such a betrayal, but that her sensi-
tive conscience made her blame herself, on subsequent
reflection, to a very exaggerated extent. To sum up the
whole complicated matter, it is clear that Joan, distraught
and bewildered, was coerced into signing, conditionally
upon the fulfillment of certain promises which were afterwards broken, and stating *at the time* (as the French
minute tells us) that she subscribed "only in so far as it
pleased our Lord," to some short form of recantation, the
exact contents of which we shall never know. Whereas the
official record, omitting all mention of disorder, threats,
promises, or conditions, represents her as having repeated and signed a much longer form. This fact alone is
sufficient to destroy the fable of Cauchon's good faith.

Why, it may be asked, did Cauchon desire an abjuration? Certainly he not only wanted it but expected it,

since (as the record itself states) he had had a form prepared, and his consultation of Cardinal Beaufort as to what was to be done after Joan's submission was therefore a mere formality.

In the first place, an abjuration would make Joan appear to have lost the courage of her convictions, to the great damage of her prestige. An abjuration, moreover, *if followed by a relapse,* made Joan's doom absolutely certain; a relapsed heretic had no further legal hope, but was perforce "handed over to the secular arm" for execution. Cauchon's aim was thus by hook or by crook attained. It seems, however, that though Joan would surely have retracted her "abjuration" sooner or later, her enemy was not content to wait for this, but resorted once more to trickery. Of events between the scene in the cemetery of Saint Ouen and the interview in Joan's prison, that is to say, of May 25, 26, and 27, the official record says nothing. Six witnesses at the rehabilitation, however, give highly interesting testimony concerning the happenings of these days.

The fury of the English, who supposed that Joan's "abjuration" had enabled her to escape the death penalty, continued to rage. John Beaupère, former Rector of the University of Paris, together with several other assessors, was sent by Cauchon to ascertain Joan's dispositions on May 25 or 26. They were received at the prison with threats of violence, and driven away without accomplishing their errand. The same treatment was accorded to others, including Manchon and the other recorders, on these days and the following. It was only because of special protection by the Earl of Warwick, who knew, of course, that Joan had by no means escaped her doom, that the three recorders ventured to go into the prison chamber on May 28. There they found Cauchon and several others, and the interview already described took place. Its tenor is confirmed by the rehabilitation witnesses; but important additional information is also given. Two Dominican friars, Martin Ladvenu and Isambard de la Pierre, who, though they had concurred in Joan's condemnation, showed great sympathy for her in her last hours, report that Joan herself told them that an English lord had actually tried to assault her and that for this reason she had reassumed male clothing, which afforded some measure of protection, and which, as Brother Isambard said, "had been treacherously left within her reach." Massieu reports Joan's statement somewhat differently. On May 27, he says, Joan's female clothing was forcibly removed, and male clothing dumped upon her. After a long argument with the guards, being compelled by bodily necessity to seek temporary release from her place of confinement — she was chained by her feet to a bed — she donned the only clothing available. The two statements are not necessarily contradictory, and in any case, there is no question but that male clothing *was* available. This fact alone proves that her "relapse," in its most obvious and visible aspect, was deliberately planned, as her "abjuration" had been planned, and that her doom was thus made certain. Small wonder that, as Boisguillaume says, many rejoiced at Joan's resumption of male clothing, and that, as Brother Isambard reports, Cauchon exclaimed to the Earl of Warwick: "This time she is well caught!"

8

THE FINAL DELIBERATION

ON May 29 a large number of assessors met by Cauchon's order in the archiepiscopal chapel. What happened at this last consultation is of special interest, since it casts further light on the abjuration, the accuracy of Courcelles' editing, the methods of Cauchon, and the attitude of Quicherat toward the trial.

The Bishop related at some length to the assembly his verification, on the previous day, of Joan's "relapse," and caused to be read by a notary a summary of the Maid's declarations on that occasion; i.e., the interview on May 28, dealt with in the preceding chapter. We have already seen how significantly the earlier French minute differs from Courcelles' Latin version in its account of the interview. There is a no less significant difference in the two accounts of the deliberation on May 29. For the minute (here in Latin, no doubt because the discussions were in that language) states that after the "schedule" of Joan's remarks had been read, *there was also read the schedule of abjuration* — a fact which Courcelles preferred to omit in his final version.

The Bishop then called for the opinions of the assessors present. The first to speak thought Joan a heretic, to be handed over to secular justice, with the usual and purely conventional plea for mercy. Next was the Abbot of Fécamp, a leader at the trial, and in no sense partial to the accused. He thought Joan relapsed, advised that the word of God be set forth to her, and added a most important opinion. "Let," he said, according to the minute, "the schedule recently read [*schedula nuper lecta*] be also read, that is, explained." "Nuper" is a strange word, even in medieval Latin, for "just now," for which one would expect *modo* or *proxime;* but if the Abbot meant that the document *just* read *to them* should be read *to her,* he must at any rate have been thinking of the long formula of abjuration, which, as we know from the minute, was part of what had just been read, and which, as the evidence in the previous chapter shows, Joan had never seen or heard. It is much more likely that the Abbot meant: "The document *recently* read *to her* should be read and expounded to her again." (Courcelles, though he had failed to mention the abjuration being read at the meeting, would thus be reporting the Abbot's meaning correctly as: "*ut schedula nuper lecta legatur iterum coram ipsa.*")

That being done, the Abbot added, she should be condemned. In other words, he voted, to salve his conscience, for Joan's execution, only on condition of being made certain, as he was then far from being, that she, thoroughly understanding the formula of abjuration, had canonically abjured and afterwards relapsed. Of the forty assessors who voted after the Abbot, thirty-eight adhered to his vote (most of them merely stating their agreement, though a few added that they also considered Joan a relapsed heretic). One assessor vaguely referred to "the theologians" as to what should be done, and only one omitted all reference to the Abbot's vote, thus placing himself with the assessor who had spoken first. In other words an overwhelming majority of the assessors — thirty-nine out of forty-two — were unwilling, hostile, or subservient as they were, that final sentence should be pronounced on Joan till they were sure that she had really understood and signed the formula which had been read to them. In spite of this, Cauchon ignored the vote. The last thing he wanted to do was to confront Joan with the long formula.

Quicherat recognized the importance of this. "The wish of such a large majority," he writes in his *Aperçus nouveaux*, "constituted a duty for the Bishop of Beauvais"; and he concludes that Cauchon "went to see Joan a few hours before her death, and certainly spoke to her about her retraction; for only a remonstrance on those grounds could have brought forth the words reported in the posthumous information." Now this information forms an appendix to the trial, and is, as we shall see later (Chapter 15), a very questionable document indeed. Moreover, we find therein no mention of Cauchon's reminding Joan of her abjuration. This is indeed mentioned in the later testimony of Brother John Toutmouillé; but nowhere is there any reference to Cauchon's reading and expounding the long formula to her, as he had been urged to do. And indeed Quicherat, having assumed, in his characteristic effort to give Cauchon's methods the benefit of every doubt, that the Bishop *did* do as the assessors advised, seems conscious of the weakness of his position. "Why," he asks, as well he may, "was such an important formality not included in the judgment, since its issue was favorable to partisan hatred, for the accused persisted in her relapse; and since its omission could be charged against the Bishop of Beauvais as an infraction of the council's wishes? Why, moreover, denature it by putting it in the suspicious form of a superadded and unattested document?" (i.e., the posthumous information). His only answer is that since this point, "certainly the weakest of the Rouen trial . . . was not brought up at the rehabilitation," it is "impossible to condemn the Bishop of Beauvais on a point as to which the judges of his memory have by implication absolved him."

Here the distinguished editor unfortunately brought to the support of his gratuitous assumption an argument erroneous in fact. For the point *was* brought up at the rehabilitation, at least three times. One of many articles drawn up by the advocates at the later process against the Rouen trial reads in part as follows: "That she [Joan] did not understand the aforesaid schedule [the formula of abjuration], is sufficiently evident from the last deliberation in the trial, that of the Abbot of Fécamp and others, a majority, there as consultors, who all said that she should be questioned as to her understanding of it. Nevertheless, *nothing of the sort was done.*" The Promoter of the Cause at the rehabilitation makes, in his "requisition," essentially the same charge. Finally, Bréhal, one of the judges on the rehabilitation tribunal, and official summarizer of the whole process in his *Recollectio,* remarks concerning the alleged relapse, that "the aforesaid bishop, not acquiescing in the decision and advice of the sounder portion of the assistants called together by him on the case, swiftly and precipitously proceeded to the definitive sentence."

Quicherat, who paid little attention to the *Recollectio,* of which he published only brief extracts, may well have missed this passage, but he should have remembered the other two, which are printed in his own edition.

9

VICTORY

ON May 30, as on May 24, a large and distinguished group of clergy, including Joan's judges, were seated on a platform to hear her preached at. This time, however, the place was the square of the Old Market of Rouen; this time the preacher was Doctor Nicholas Midi, author of the twelve articles, whose sentiments concerning the crimes of the accused were the same as those of Doctor William Érart, though his text was different; this time, above all, the proceedings could only end in one way. There was therefore, another elevation besides the platform on which the clerical and lay dignitaries sat, and that on which Joan stood to be harangued. It was a mass of plaster, topped by faggots and a stake. On the stake was a placard inscribed with the words: "Heretic, Relapse, Apostate, Idolater." After the sermon came an exhortation to repentance and submission preached by Cauchon; then two long sentences were read, the first proclaiming Joan's relapse, the second a repetition of the sentence of excommunication which she had interrupted on May 24.

The official account ends with these sentences; but from the somewhat confused recollections of the rehabilitation witnesses, our primary source of information concerning the actual execution, we learn many details. Joan confessed to Brother Martin Ladvenu and received Communion in her cell that morning. (Other happenings there will be discussed in the next chapter.) Clad in female dress, she was led by soldiers, of whom seven or eight hundred were present, to the place of execution, weeping and calling on God and her saints. The populace were also in tears and murmured against the judgment. The churchmen withdrew, according to custom, after the sentence had been read, only Martin Ladvenu and Isambard de la Pierre remaining till the end. When Joan asked for a cross, a soldier improvised one for her from his staff; she still begged a cross from a church, till from the church of St. Saviour near by one was brought her, which she embraced with tears. Then, without the formality of a secular sentence, though the civil authorities were present, she was led to the stake by the executioner. The record does not state whether or not there was put on her head at this moment the grotesque "miter" of parchment painted with devils, usually worn by condemned heretics. As the faggots were lit, the Maid begged Brother Isambard to go down, and still to hold the cross before her eyes. She died with a last loud cry of "Jesus!"

The English caused her ashes to be thrown into the Seine. Yet many of them were shaken. Brother Isambard says that the executioner exclaimed to him in despair: "I greatly fear that I shall be damned. I have burned a saint!" And he related that, in spite of all his efforts, her heart had remained unconsumed.

10

THE POSTHUMOUS INFORMATION

TO the official account of the Rouen trial certain documents are appended. They include letters, which attempt, with much sanctimonious verbiage, to vindicate the trial and its verdict, written in the name of the boy King Henry VI to the Emperor and all Christian princes, and to the nobles and cities of "his kingdom of France"; also a letter of similar tenor from the University of Paris to the Pope, the Emperor, and the College of Cardinals; and, curiously enough, the retraction and sentence to imprisonment of a Dominican friar who had been rash enough to criticize the Rouen verdict.

More important than these letters, however, is a document which precedes them, consisting of sworn depositions made to the judges by seven of the assessors, one week after Joan's execution, and professing to report statements made by Joan on the morning of her execution. These constitute the famous "Posthumous Information," concerning which, as concerning the abjuration, much controversy has raged. With some variations, these depositions represent Joan as having retracted her "relapse," that is to say, as having admitted that her voices had after all deceived her, since they had not delivered her, and as having agreed that they were from evil spirits, or at least declared her willingness to accept the decision of churchmen in the matter. She is also reported as admitting that her account of having seen an angel bringing a crown to the Dauphin — an obscure matter of which she had spoken with extreme reluctance, apparent inconsistency, and possible allegorizing, during the trial — was fictitious; she herself was the angel. One deponent tells of her making sacramental confession to Brother Martin Ladvenu at that time, and receiving Communion from his hands.

Concerning these events we have considerable testimony given at the royal investigation which began the rehabilitation. Ladvenu confirms the fact that, with Cauchon's authorization, he administered the sacraments to Joan on May 30; he states that on that morning the bishop and several canons came to see Joan; but he also reports as does Brother John Toutmouillé (another Dominican assessor whose alleged deposition, like Ladvenu's, is in the Posthumous Information) that Joan on that occasion bitterly reproached Cauchon for leaving her in her enemies' hands and for being the cause of her death. Far from mentioning any new retractions or admissions, however, Ladvenu declared in 1456 that "up to the end of her life she maintained and affirmed that the voices she had heard came to her from God; that all she had done had been at God's command; that she did not believe that her voices had deceived her."

Now the Posthumous Information, like the documents which follow it, forms no part of the judicial record. In the three original manuscripts, all these appendices follow the elaborate attestations of the three notaries and the seals of the judges. Nor do their pages bear the signature of any notary, as all the previous pages of the record do. Moreover, one of the notaries, namely Manchon, testified at the royal investigation of 1450, that he had refused, in spite of pressure by Cauchon, to attest the Posthumous Information, and his fellow notaries seem to have taken the same stand. Manchon gives as the reason for his refusal the fact that he was not present at the conversation, but, though his unwillingness to attest those pages does not, of course, disprove the allegations they report, it does emphasize their extrajudicial character. And the very different accounts of the scene given by Ladvenu and Toutmouillé make the depositions published by Cauchon seem highly suspicious. Even without contrary evidence it is scarcely credible that Joan should have begged pardon of the English and Burgundians for fighting them and causing them to be slain, as Canon Loyseleur (Joan's implacable enemy) describes her as doing.

We know from Ladvenu and Toutmouillé that there was an interview between Cauchon and Joan on the morning of her execution, after she had received the sacraments. Surely Cauchon tried his best to make her disavow her voices at this time, since a second abjuration, he supposed, would be a final blow to her prestige, and involved no risk of her escaping the stake, after she had once relapsed. Indeed the desire to strike such a blow is the only possible motive for adding the Posthumous Information to the record of the trial. The desire is again manifested in the letters mentioned at the beginning of this chapter, though the second abjuration is there inconsistently placed (the letters were no doubt written earlier) just before Joan's death, after a secular verdict — which was never rendered!

Threatened and terrified on the morning of her execution, the Maid may have uttered words which Cauchon could twist to his purposes, but the evidence that she spoke as reported is dubious indeed. Speculation on the amount of truth in the reports is therefore greatly influenced by the opinion of a given historian as to whether

Cauchon is more, or less, likely to have invented or tampered with the depositions than Ladvenu is to have perjured himself at the rehabilitation by contradicting them.

11

REPARATION BEGINS

I N 1433, two years after the Maid's death, La Trémoïlle was assassinated. The King now turned to more energetic advisers, prominent among whom were Arthur de Richemont, Constable of France, and Dunois, the Bastard of Orleans, Joan's devoted friend. A peace with Burgundy was concluded at Arras in 1435, the year in which the Duke of Bedford died. Richemont entered Paris, followed shortly by the King, in 1436. A revolt broke out in Poitou, in 1440, but was successfully quelled. In 1444 a truce was made with England, and a regular army organized; but it was not till 1449 that the conquest of Normandy began. A force under Dunois was at the walls of Rouen in October of that year, and Charles made a solemn entry on November 10. In the description of the elaborate pageantry which accompanied this event, there is no reference to the Maid. An amnesty was proclaimed in favor of all who had been active during the English occupation. Charles then marched on Harfleur with Dunois and a large force. After the town surrendered on December 24, the King joined Agnes Sorel, who had been his mistress for several years, at Jumièges. She died soon after.

Then, after nearly nineteen years, Charles finally made a move to clear Joan's memory. On February 15, 1450, a royal rescript was issued from Rouen to William Bouillé, Doctor of Theology, Dean of the Cathedral of Noyon, and former Rector of the University of Paris, directing him to start an investigation of the Rouen trial. During the following month Bouillé interviewed seven witnesses, namely, the friars Isambard de la Pierre, John Tout-mouillé, Martin Ladvenu, and William Duval, the notary Manchon, the bailiff Massieu, and Master John Beaupère, always hostile to Joan, who still thought she had been "very subtle, with a woman's subtlety." Bouillé also composed a memoir, the first to be written (after Gerson's, written during Joan's life) of those included in the dossier of the rehabilitation. In its original form, this memoir states as its purpose, not only the glory of God, but also "the exaltation of the King of the French, that is, the House of France, which has never been reported to have favored heretics or to have adhered to them in any way."

There is no evidence that efforts were made at this time to secure the authorization of Pope Nicholas V for the revision of the trial. If such were made, the Pope was no doubt too susceptible to Anglo-Burgundian influence to respond, at least until the conclusion of a permanent peace between France and England.

It was to start negotiations for such a peace that William, Cardinal d'Estouteville, was sent to France as papal legate in the summer of 1451. This prelate, of a noble Norman house, was a relative of Charles VII; his brother had shared in the supposedly impossible feat of capturing Mont Saint Michel from the English in 1425. The Cardinal, who had lived for many years at Rome, was a patriotic Frenchman. Though he followed the scandalous fashion of his time in amassing numerous benefices, he was in many ways an admirable and energetic man, and the author of wise reforms at the University of Paris. In the spring of 1452 he went to Rouen (he was later to be its archbishop), where, either on his own initiative or in obedience to a papal or royal suggestion, "because of current rumors and many other things which have been daily reported, during the time of his legation, about the said process carried on against the said Joan," he enlisted the services of the Dominican John Bréhal, Grand Inquisitor of France, and instituted canonical proceedings for the revision.

Two Italian canonists, Theodore de Leliis and Paul Pontanus, had come with d'Estouteville from Rome. They were now furnished with the relevant documents, namely the Rouen record, Bouillé's memoir, and the seven depositions made to him. Since, however, these depositions, not having formed part of an ecclesiastical process, were without canonical standing, the Legate and the Inquisitor proceeded to take new ones at Rouen, on the basis of a questionnaire of twelve articles. Three of the five witnesses now heard, Manchon, de la Pierre, and Ladvenu, had testified to Bouillé in 1450.

After d'Estouteville had been summoned to Paris, Bréhal called twelve more witnesses, who were interrogated on a longer questionnaire, as were the five who had deposed shortly before. Of the new witnesses, only the bailiff Massieu had testified to Bouillé; the others included Taquel, recorder at Rouen for the Vice-Inquisitor Lemaître, several assessors, and others who had special knowledge of the trial. The results of this investigation were submitted by Bréhal to d'Estouteville in Paris. With their way prepared by a letter from the Legate to the King, the Inquisitor and Bouillé then journeyed to the castle in Touraine where Charles was amusing himself. Passing through Orleans, they were officially greeted by the city as vindicators of the Maid.

The King realized the necessity of securing papal authority as soon as possible for the further conduct of the

affair. At the Legate's advice, he directed Bréhal to continue his work in the meantime by the consultation of still
more theologians and canonists whose opinions would
carry weight. He also provided funds for the expenses involved. For the guidance of those to be consulted, the Inquisitor drew up a résumé known as the *Summarium*.
This document, from which only very brief extracts were
published by Quicherat, contains no legal arguments or
criticisms of the trial, but summarizes the charges against
Joan and such of her statements as are relevant to them.
It is based on an admirably thorough and objective study
of the Rouen record, and ends with the words: "These are
the points concerning which it would seem that deliberations should be held at present."

In the autumn of 1452 d'Estouteville returned to Rome
in obedience to a papal summons, accompanied, no
doubt, by de Leliis and Pontanus. Before leaving France,
the two canonists composed memoirs on the trial; each
wrote another such memoir in Rome sometime later. Six
more memoirs composed before the end of 1453 are ex-
tant, four of which were included in the official dossier of
the rehabilitation. All are by French doctors. Of the
whole collection of memoirs, Quicherat edited only two
in full, though he gave brief extracts from the rest, except
for one, which he may not have known.

The Pope's failure to act on the material submitted to
him now held up the proceeding for two years. The vast
problems created by the fall of Constantinople are sufficient to account for this. The sovereigns of Christendom
reacted variously to the papal effort to organize a crusade
against Turkish aggression, and the Pope probably hesitated lest Anglo-French relations be further complicated
by a renewed discussion of the Rouen verdict under papal
auspices.

Finally, Bréhal adopted a suggestion which had been made by one of the memorialists, John de Montigny, Doctor of Canon Law at the University of Paris. It was that Joan's mother and two surviving brothers should petition the Holy See for the continuation of the process of revision by the appointment of a commission with authority to annul the verdict of 1431. Such a plea was, therefore, drawn up in the name of Joan's relatives, and taken to Rome, probably by Bréhal, in 1454. By leaving Charles VII out of the picture and making the process a private one, Joan's friends had found a way to avoid the danger of political consequences. The plea, which attacks the trial on several counts, and calls for justice against the Rouen judges and the prosecutor d'Estivet, all now deceased, refers to Cauchon as *bonae memoriae,* "of good memory." Since this has been taken as implying approbation of the Bishop of Beauvais, it is well to point out that it is a purely formal phrase, used of any bishop who had died in communion with Rome, unless his acts had been juridically condemned.

Nicholas V died in March, 1455, apparently without taking any steps in the affair. His successor, Calixtus III (Alphonsus Borgia) was elected in April, at the age of seventy-seven years. Of a firm and uncompromising character, he lost no time in responding favorably to the plea of Isabelle d'Arc and her sons. By a rescript dated June 11, 1455, he gave full powers to deal with and decide the matter to three well-chosen members of the French hierarchy: John Juvenal des Ursins, Archbishop of Rheims; William Chartier, Bishop of Paris; and Richard Oliver de Longueil, Bishop of Coutances. They were authorized to act either separately or together, and were bidden to add "an inquisitor" to their tribunal. Of course, they chose John Bréhal.

12

A CLOUD OF WITNESSES

THE commission now formed under direct papal authority held its first solemn hearing in the Cathedral of Notre Dame in Paris on the morning of November 7, 1455. Longueil being absent till the following June on a diplomatic mission to Burgundy, des Ursins, Chartier, and Bréhal were seated at the gates of the choir. Up the long nave came Joan's mother, clothed in mourning, and bearing in her hand the papal rescript. She was accompanied by her two sons, a group of citizens of Orleans, and many others. Groaning and weeping, she fell on her knees before the papal commissioners to voice her plea. Several learned clerics spoke in her support. Soon the sympathetic murmurs of the crowd became so disturbing that the judges led Isabelle to the sacristy, where, after formally accepting the papal mandate, they warned her of the difficulties involved in the process, which she declared herself resolved to face with confidence in the justice of her cause.

After fulfilling several necessary legal formalities in Paris, the judges ordered all interested parties to appear before them in Rouen in December. The Bishop of Beauvais and his prosecutor, besides the Vice-Inquisitor of that diocese, were especially summoned to defend the actions of their predecessors, Cauchon, d'Estivet, and Lemaître. Proxies were appointed to represent Isabelle d'Arc and her sons, who were excused from going to Rouen. Served with the summonses, the Bishop and his prosecutor merely replied that they had no interest in the proceedings, while the Dominican prior at Beauvais declared that he knew of no inquisitorial officer in that diocese. Apparently there had never been such an officer, since, as the judges, of course, knew from the record, Lemaître belonged in Rouen, and had been specially authorized by his superior to act with Cauchon. Indeed the only person to respond to the summons at this time was a representative of Cauchon's heirs, who protested that they had no intention of defending the Rouen trial; but, anxious lest their interests should suffer in consequence of the new process, appealed to the amnesty granted by Charles VII after his conquest of Normandy.

Ten witnesses, all of whom had deposed in 1452, were again heard at Rouen. On December 20, Simon Chapitault, promoter of the cause, summarized the defects of the Rouen trial in a speech before the judges. He urged that further investigations be made, and asked especially that an inquiry into Joan's life and morals be conducted in the region of her origin. The court then adjourned for the required Christmas recess, which was spent in Paris.

Four witnesses were heard there in January. They included Tiphaine and Delachambre, two medical doctors who had attended Joan at Rouen, and who gave interesting data on other matters concerning the trial. The other two were John de Mailly, Bishop of Noyon, and Thomas de Courcelles. These wholehearted abettors of Cauchon testified reluctantly, and, in Courcelles' case, far from frankly. (See page 4.)

The inquiry in Joan's native region began late in January. A similar inquiry had, as the law required, been held by Cauchon in 1431, but as its results were entirely favorable to the Maid, had been omitted from the record after having been read to a few assessors. In 1456, thirty-four witnesses were interviewed at Domrémy, Vaucouleurs, and Toul, on the basis of a questionnaire of twelve articles. A summary of their invaluable testimony has been given in the third chapter.

When the sessions at Rouen were resumed on February 16, the Beauvais prosecutor, one Master Reginald Bredouille, finally roused by repeated summonses, appeared, and was invited to contest the one-hundred-one articles that had been drawn up against the trial. He denied, as indeed his function required, the cogency of the allegations, and, for vindication of the trial, simply referred to the Rouen record. He added that neither he nor his bishop intended to intervene further in the matter, but willingly left everything in the judges' hands. The Dominican prior of Évreux appeared on the same day, complained of the embarrassment caused to his brethren of Beauvais by the summonses, and protested that no inquisitor or vice-inquisitor had resided in their priory for many years. (We have seen that Lemaître belonged in Rouen.) In spite of these protestations, the commissioners, careful to observe every possible legal requirement, decided to continue the sending of summonses to the parties concerned, and finally declared them "contumacious."

Des Ursins, accompanied by William Bouillé (the royal commissioner in 1450, now officially associated with the tribunal) and by a representative of Bréhal, then started an inquiry at Orleans, where a long and important deposition was made by Count de Dunois, who was followed by a large number of townsfolk.

Chartier and Bréhal, in Paris, were for some months occupied by other urgent duties. Early in April they heard once more the four witnesses who had deposed in

January. Among others heard were Joan's page, Louis de Contes, and Gobert Thibault, her squire. After des Ursin's return to Paris, the Duke of Alençon and twelve others were heard, including John Pasquerel, Joan's chaplain, who made a written statement. Among four witnesses heard soon afterward at Rouen was the Dominican Séguin de Séguin, who gave highly important testimony on the questioning of the Maid at Poitiers in 1429. (See Chapter 3.)

The final testimony to be received was a long statement, the only one which appears in the record in its original French, made at Lyons and duly attested, by John d'Aulon, who had been specially entrusted with Joan's welfare by the King, and was her steward and constant companion during most of her military career. Like the Maid's other fellows in arms, d'Aulon bore eloquent testimony to her purity as well as to her military genius.

Thus ended the series of one-hundred-fourteen witnesses (not counting the six who testified in 1450 or 1452 only) called to tell what they knew of Joan's life and especially of her trial. The zeal, thoroughness, and meticulous regard for legal correctness which the papal commissioners had shown in the execution of their huge task are evident from this account, though I have omitted to mention many meetings of a purely formal character. While there is — perhaps to avoid emphasizing her King's neglect — an almost complete absence of testimony concerning the last months of the Maid's career as a soldier, and of those during which she was a prisoner, we should remember that the commissioners' sole aim was to review Joan's trial, not to supply material for her future biographers.

It hardly needs to be said that the judges thoroughly studied and discussed the theological memoirs which had been drawn up for them, besides the one composed by the Chancellor Gerson in Joan's lifetime. In fact they caused two more memoirs to be written in the spring of 1456. Early in June, the period during which any of the testimony received could be contested was declared to have expired, and the whole vast mass of documentation was formally recognized as the official material of the process. Yet it seemed advisable to the commissioners, before pronouncing judgment, to have a complete, exhaustive, and entirely official recapitulation of the defects which had been urged against the Rouen trial, as of the opinions expressed by the memorialists. No one could be so well equipped for this task, both because of his personal qualifications and of his position on their own papal tribunal, as John Bréhal. He set to work at once, and the result was the *Recollectio*.

13

CRITICS AND THE "RECOLLECTIO"

A WORK more successful in fulfilling its purpose than Bréhal's great study of Joan's trial can hardly be imagined. It has nevertheless been criticized by many historians of the Maid. Thus, Edmond Richer, in the seventeenth century, found it, along with the other memoirs, "insufficiently wrought and polished, and tumultuously written, even for a century when barbarism was triumphant." Fabre reproached it for dullness, for failure to give new facts about Joan, and for lack of enthusiasm. Quicherat excused himself for publishing only brief extracts of this and of most of the other memoirs on the ground that "there is nothing historical about them."

These criticisms are either beside the point or untrue. Bréhal was not Cicero, but he wrote clear and sometimes eloquent scholastic Latin, however much he may have failed to satisfy the exigencies of pseudo-classic elegance. It is unreasonable to ask that a painstaking analysis, theological and canonical, of the Rouen trial, should be other than technical in its language and austerely legal in its approach; that it should furnish new biographical facts, which had been abundantly supplied by the testimony; or that it should interrupt its argument to engage in eloquent panegyrics — though, as a matter of fact, its author's warm admiration for the Maid is constantly evident. Finally, it is absurd to deny the *historical* importance of the *Recollectio,* if Joan's orthodoxy and the legality of the trial are, among other things, historical questions. For surely the best solution of these questions must come from theologians and canonists, and the more nearly contemporary such experts are, the better. After all, Bréhal knew more about inquisitorial procedure in his own day than Quicherat or any nineteenth-century historian, not to mention Mr. Shaw; and if modern scholars are too incompetent, or too bored, to make a thorough study of the *Recollectio*, they must expect the charge of neglecting data absolutely essential for answering the aforesaid questions.

Were it possible to doubt the complete moral integrity of Bréhal and his fellow commissioners, which Quicherat grants, the situation would, of course, be quite different. Insinuations of that sort, however, are entirely derived from the presuppositions I have mentioned; namely, that Joan was a heretic, that the trial was therefore essentially legal, and hence that the rehabilitation verdict must have been determined by political influences. Now there is no shred of evidence of such influences, at least after the investigation was taken over by the Holy See. Of course, the King wanted Joan vindicated, and he was paying the costs of the process. The commissioners were no doubt predisposed in her favor, but to imply that they therefore dealt with the evidence in any other than a completely objective way is quite gratuitously unfair to them, and contradicts the whole tenor of the *Recollectio*. For had there been any need of soft-pedaling the question of Joan's orthodoxy because of anything that she had said, the *Recollectio* would have been a very different document. It could have condemned the Rouen trial on various conclusive grounds, and if necessary excused Joan because of her lack of knowledge. The *Recollectio*, however, does far more than this. Bréhal therein supports every work of Joan's, especially, as we shall see, in regard to the question of submission to the Church. Now can anyone imagine that a Grand Inquisitor, composing under direct papal authority the most important official opinion of his career, could afford to support statements even remotely savoring of heresy? If he had been so rash, would the judges have made the *Recollectio* the immediate basis of their verdict, or would the Pope have accepted this verdict? Finally, would the Holy See, at the canonization of Joan in 1920, have endorsed the rehabilitation, or indeed have canonized Joan at all? The conclusion is unavoidable that if the Maid was a "Protestant," so was the Grand Inquisitor John Bréhal, so were his fellow commissioners, so was Calixtus III, and so was Benedict XV — which is surely too paradoxical a statement even for Mr. Shaw! Moreover, as Bréhal's vindication of Joan must be accepted as in accordance with the strictest Catholic orthodoxy, so his criticisms of the trial have an equal claim to be considered valid in terms of the ecclesiastical law of the period. His reputation here also was at stake; he could not afford to make captious objections. It is perfectly safe, therefore, to conclude that the defects he alleges were really such.

The *Recollectio* shows, of course, what might be called the theological accents of its time, especially in the number, and sometimes the content, of its quotations from a long list of authors, sacred and classical. Yet, though some of its minor arguments would not be used by modern Catholic theologians, the work as a whole remains, and must always remain, the final word on the iniquity of Joan's trial and on her unwavering loyalty to the Church.

Finally, it should be remembered that, since the *Recol-*

lectio depends on the official record of the Rouen trial
far more than on the rehabilitation testimony, its conclusions are not essentially affected by criticism of the latter,
even when justified.

14

THE MATTER OF THE TRIAL

IN a short introduction, after discussing man's natural tendency, and duty, to embrace truth and to hate falsehood, Bréhal states his conviction, subject to the decision of the Holy See, that Joan's trial wrought vast harm to truth, both in the "justice" administered by the so-called judges, and in the doctrine expressed by those who assisted. He proposes to treat the subject under two main headings: the matter of the trial; and the manner of its procedure.

The following résumé, though greatly condensed from the nine long chapters of the first part, will give an accurate idea of their substance.

1. *The Visions*

Bréhal's direct aim is not to establish the supernatural origin of Joan's visions, though his belief in the matter is evident, but rather to show the lack of foundation for the condemnation which they incurred. He discusses in great detail, and with an abundance of quotations from Scripture and the Doctors of the Church, the time and place at which the apparitions began, their character, and their effect on Joan. Their entire lack of any reprehensible feature is his argument for their divine origin.

2. *The Revelations*

Following, as he constantly does, St. Thomas Aquinas,

Bréhal states that supposed private revelations must ʾ
tested by the character of their recipient (though G
occasionally sends them to his enemies, as in the case
Belshazzar), his purpose, and the certitude which ͭ
engender in him. Joan faithfully obeyed the prompt
to piety and virtue which her revelations brou· ιt, ·ſ
purpose was not vainglory but a noble one, nar   e
welfare of France, and her certitude points to th ·ᴅ ιe
origin.

3. *Joan's Prophecies*

True prophecy must be entirely fulfilled, God ·ʋ   n-
struct the prophet when its meaning is not ob·ᴊ   it
must contain nothing contrary to faith or morals,   ιe
prophet must clearly recognize that his knowleᵈ   is
divinely revealed. Now most of Joan's prophecⁱ·ᴊ   ιt
she would deliver Orleans, be wounded there ᴸᴀvᵩ e
King crowned at Rheims, and, at an unknown t   e
captured, besides many others, were all fulfilled
There is a difficulty in regard to her predictⁱᵒn   t
she would deliver the Duke of Orleans from his ι ᴊι ·ſ
in England; but, as she explained, she meant ι
would free him within three years, if she lived th ·lᶜ
Also, her voices told her that she would be fre· ɦᴑıı
prison, and would have a great victory; but — the   ᴊ·ᴇr-
ward told her not to be anxious at her martyrdom, since
she would go to heaven, thus interpreting their own
prophecy in a mystical sense. Besides, there is an imper-
fect sort of prophetic communication which is not wholly
understood, and the prophet (whose inspiration is tran-
sient) may also speak as a mere fallible human. So that
even if Joan had made unverified predictions (which is
not admitted) this would be no disproof of her occa-
sional inspiration.

4. *Joan's Homage to the Apparitions*

Since Joan did not share the popular superstitions concerning the "fairy tree" and its adjacent fountain (in spite of what was said at the trial), though she did hear her voices there at least once, her homage and its manifestations were irreproachably in accord with Catholic doctrine and practice concerning the veneration of the saints. What she asked of these saints was altogether laudable. Such being her dispositions, her mistake would not have been dangerous even if the visions had been really evil spirits, whose aid she always abhorred. "It is a marvel," Bréhal exclaims, "how she could be accused, on these grounds, of idolatry or of consorting with demons!"

5. *Joan's Conduct Toward Her Parents*

Filial piety (concerning which Bréhal quotes from Cicero and Seneca!) cannot impose obligations contrary to God's will. Prudence prevented Joan from divulging her divine mission to her parents, who might have interfered. In all else she was obedient, and she even asked and obtained pardon for her one necessary disobedience.

6. *Joan's Wearing of Male Clothing*

Joan's motive in wearing male clothing — in itself a morally indifferent thing — was good, namely to safeguard her own chastity and that of others. Biblical and other legislation does not apply in this exceptional case. The judges lied when they said she had rather not receive Communion than abandon her male attire, since she often asked for a long dress for this purpose. As for her standard, arms, and taking part in battles, *those* were the things which aroused the judges' hatred, Bréhal ironically remarks. Yet she reluctantly obeyed her voices in taking up arms, she bore her standard so as to avoid slaying anyone, which she never did, and she was always merciful to those captured. She was not sinning in her warlike actions, any more than were Deborah, Jael, and Judith.

7. Certain Statements of Joan's

She was certain with the certainty of faith that her visions and voices were from God; but — this was because of their holy teachings and promptings, which was a fully sufficient motive.

She was sure of her salvation; but — on condition that she kept her promise to God of preserving her virginity of body and soul.

She wished the head of a certain Burgundian cut off; but — only if it pleased God. (The Burgundian, incidentally, had a fair trial on charges of murder, robbery, and treachery. His execution was legal.)

She was much harried for saying that she had seen an angel coming to the King; but — this was a great mystery pertaining to the safety of the kingdom, about which she had a right to speak with prudence and in parables.

She was charged with saying that she had never committed a mortal sin; but — this is false. When asked if she were in a state of grace, she replied, "very Catholically and humbly": "If I be not, God bring me to it; if I be, God keep me in it."

She declared that she had *damned* herself to save her life, by abjuring; but — she may have meant that she had *condemned* herself to death. If she referred to a sin committed by abjuring through fear (which is never lawful in regard to revealed truth), it may, indeed, be impossible to excuse her completely, but one must bear in mind the terrible sufferings she had endured, the lying promises and other tricks used to make her abjure, and her fear of death. "Words uttered in such trepidation are not to be imputed."

8. *Submission to the Church*

The eighth chapter of Bréhal's *Recollectio* is of prime importance for the subject of this book. It answers thoroughly and finally the question with which I started, namely, that of Joan's fidelity to the Church. It crowns the labors and anticipates the verdict of the papal commissioners who so admirably conducted the rehabilitation. In connection with the whole treatise, whereof it forms the most important section, it is really the first argument in the process which, resumed four centuries later, culminated in the canonization of the Maid.

Bréhal begins his study of the "sly and lengthy hunting" by which Joan's enemies sought to ensnare her on the question of submission to the Church with a discussion of what the simple faithful are bound to believe.

Turning to Joan's case, he notes the difficulty, nay, ambiguity, of the question asked her; i.e., whether she would submit her words and deeds to the judgment of the Church. Her words chiefly concerned the apparitions, revelations, and prophecies, which have already been amply dealt with; her deeds had to do with civil polity, the raising up of the kingdom of France and the expulsion of its enemies. *Neither words nor deeds of Joan involve the primary or secondary doctrines of the Faith, but are rather concerned with pious beliefs about which the faithful are free to differ. Therefore she could not err dangerously if she did not submit.*

Moreover, she always maintained that her words and deeds came from divine revelation, and this brings liberty, according to the texts: "Where is the Spirit of God, there is liberty," and: "If ye are led by the Spirit, ye are not under the law." A prelate, or any man whatever, who gives commands contrary to God's law or His secret inspirations, must not be obeyed. This is what Joan meant when she said she would submit to the Church and the Pope, "God served first." *She could not, without the sin of infidelity, deny her revelations.* When she said she would obey "unless something impossible were commanded," that "it was impossible for her to revoke what she had done on God's behalf," and that "what God ordered she would not fail to do for any living man, or for anything whatever," she was by no means at fault, but spoke most correctly (*rectissime dixit*). If she had denied the certainty she had from revelation, she would have been guilty of lying and perjury.

It may be noted that, in a similar argument, the memoir of William Bouillé uses equally strong language. If Joan had denied her revelations, he says, "she would have sinned against her conscience, which was well informed by a good inspiration of this sort. This would be true even if there remained a doubt as to whether this inspiration was from a good or an evil spirit. Since this is entirely hidden and known to God alone, and consequently the Church does not judge in these matters, in which she may err, she reserves the judgment to God and leaves it to the individual conscience. Certainly, therefore, the said Maid did not err, if she submitted herself to God alone."

This passage of Bouillé's was quoted by Joan's advocate, in vindication of her stand, and in reply to the objections of the Promoter of the Faith (popularly known as "the Devil's Advocate"), in 1903, during the process of beatification.

Returning to the *Recollectio*, we find Bréhal next pointing out that distinguished clerics had for three weeks examined Joan at Poitiers. In those matters in which they had found no evil, she could speak all the more licitly and firmly, nor did she have any duty of renouncing them at the behest of others, especially as the Church of Beauvais has no superiority to the Church of Poitiers.

The word *Church* has various meanings, which Joan could not be expected to distinguish, nor was she aided by the doctors' talk of the Church militant and the Church triumphant. The question of submission was put to her in a most difficult and threatening manner, absurd, impious, and inhuman, which ill accorded with the proper procedure of an ecclesiastical court. Here was a simple country girl, skilled only in tending flocks, in weaving, and in sewing, and thinking of the "church" primarily as the material building. She might well have been excused had she not answered properly, which, however, she did. Notably, she showed her proper concept of the Church's unity: "It seems to me that it is the same with the Church as with God, and that there should be no difficulty about that. Why do you make a difficulty about it?"

Joan declared her belief that the Church is kept from error by the Holy Ghost, and stated that she was a good Christian. Let churchmen examine her answers, she said, and if they found anything contrary to the faith, she would cast it out. To the objection that clerics at Paris and elsewhere *had* condemned many of her words and deeds, Bréhal answers that the report made to them was truncated and corrupted, as he will show later; and, of course, by "clerics" Joan meant impartial ones, not partisans of the English. She asked that churchmen on the French side should also be present.

When questioned about rival claimants to the Papacy she replied correctly that she would obey the Pope who was at Rome, and asked repeatedly to be taken to him and to the General Council. From all of which it is evident that she submitted duly and sufficiently to the Church where it was her duty, and cleared herself from all note of error. Those who questioned her, however, obviously meant, not the Roman or Universal Church, but themselves, thereby showing contempt for the Pope and doing grave injury to the Holy See. "I do not see," Bréhal concludes, "how that bishop and his abettors can be excused from manifest malice against the Roman Church, or even from heresy."

9. *The Relapse*

After saying that he will deal later with Joan's "abjuration," Bréhal justifies on three grounds her resumption of male clothing. First, she had been told to wear this clothing by divine revelation, and rightly feared that her abandonment of it, without special instructions from her voices, might have been gravely sinful. Secondly, the need of protecting her chastity was increased by attacks that had been made on her. Thirdly, natural necessity forced her to leave her prison, and, according to some witnesses, only male clothing had been left with her.

In a passage vibrant with indignation Bréhal next describes the "unbridled madness" of English rejoicing at the discovery of Joan's relapse, and her modest reserve in the face of her persecutors' fury, which only emphasizes their malice. All this could not have happened without fraud, for how could she, being closely shackled, have sought clothing elsewhere?

As to her reaffirmation of her apparitions and revelations, she never intended to abjure them, not having understood the formula of abjuration. Violence was resorted to in bidding her abjure. Whatever she did was done through terror of being burned.

She is reported to have finally renounced her voices on the day of her death. Bréhal makes the obvious objections to these reports (the Posthumous Information, see Chapter 10); namely, the contradiction of them by later witnesses and their extrajudicial and unauthenticated character. In any case, he adds, it is not to be wondered at, if perhaps, after a long and cruel captivity, and terrified by threats, this tender girl wavered. Christ Himself complained that God had forsaken Him. Joan no doubt referred herself to God and the Church, but that she ever renounced her voices is not proved.

After a moving description of Joan's death, Bréhal concludes that one deluded by evil spirits would scarcely have died thus piously.

15

THE MANNER OF THE TRIAL

IN the second part of the *Recollectio,* Bréhal turns to
the manner in which Joan's trial was conducted. Concerning this, Brother Isambard de la Pierre had testified to the commissioners that the judges "observed the
order of law well enough (*satis*)," a phrase seized on by
Quicherat as the only support he could find in the rehabilitation testimony for his view that the trial was legal
and regular. Of course, the word *satis* here has the same
much weakened meaning as its English equivalent, and
merely refers to the screen of legality behind which Cauchon tried to hide his many irregularities, just so far as
there was no danger of his aim being frustrated. Indeed
Isambard goes on to say that "as to their [the judges']
inclination, they proceeded in the malice of vengeance"
— words which Quicherat did not quote.

1. *Incompetence of the Judge*

Bréhal first points out that Joan had no domicile in
Cauchon's diocese of Beauvais, or anywhere but in her
place of origin. Since, moreover, she had been examined
by a number of prelates at Poitiers, Cauchon had no right
to pass judgment against their verdict, which was at least
not unfavorable. Joan could not have committed the alleged offenses in Cauchon's diocese, since she had never
entered it until the day she was captured. Nor did her
bearing arms and wearing male clothing furnish any

basis for charges of heresy, schism, and so forth. If Cauchon had been driven out of his diocese, he might legitimately have tried a case elsewhere, but he left Beauvais of his own accord, fleeing from his lawful sovereign, as other bishops in cities taken from the English did not do. The trial should have been conducted in a place that was "safe" (for the accused), which Rouen, "subject to the English tyranny," certainly was not. Bréhal then alludes once more to the inscrutable character of Joan's revelations. As to such, he says, "the Church does not assume judgment, but rather leaves this to the divine judgment and the individual conscience." (Bréhal here repeats the words of Bouillé, quoted on p. 77.)

Of course, this complete demolition of Cauchon's claim to jurisdiction is sufficient by itself to prove the illegality of the trial.

2. *Cauchon's Partiality and Harshness*

In excoriating terms, Bréhal enumerates eighteen ways in which Cauchon showed that he took charge of and conducted the trial "with corrupt and inordinate bias" in favor of the English, and twenty-eight instances of his personal animosity to Joan. Among the latter is his failure to provide "lawful and kindly guides and defenders, as the difficulty of the cause, and the sex, age, and mentality of the person required, though this is willed and ordered by the clemency, not only of canon law, but also of civil law." Trials of this sort aim rather at bringing back the erring than at punishment, Bréhal concludes. "Every hatred, every rigor, and every impious severity is forbidden, most strictly and under the gravest penalties, both to prelates and to inquisitors delegated to deal with the stain of heresy."

3. *Joan's Prison and Guard*

By civil law, Joan should have had female guardians, and her cause required an ecclesiastical prison, which she often rightly called for. Though prisons are for detention, not punishment, she was thrown into one, under horrible conditions, even before she was summoned to trial. Soldiers were the last who should have guarded her. They treated her brutally and remained unpunished.

4. *Joan's Rejection of Her Judge, and Her Appeal*

The obviously mortal enmity of Cauchon gave Joan ample grounds for refusing to accept him as her judge. This, and the nature of her cause fully justified the appeals to the Sovereign Pontiff, which she repeatedly made, though ignorant of the correct terms. Such appeals could be lawfully denied only to one whose heresy is proved. Those who denied them erred gravely in usurping judgment after the appeal had been made.

5. *The Vice-Inquisitor*

Whether or not Lemaître was a competent judge in the case, at any rate he protested that he had no power to function for the Ordinary of Beauvais, yet Cauchon arbitrarily forced him to take part. Lacking authority, the Vice-Inquisitor could not give valid consent to Cauchon's proceeding with the case, nor does his subsequent reception of authority from his superior alter this fact. Besides, from January 9 till March 13, the Bishop acted alone, and hence with at least doubtful validity. Whatever Lemaître did afterward seems to have been done against his own conscience, through fear of the English.

6. *The Twelve Articles*

Space is lacking to follow Bréhal in the calm and masterly analysis by which he shows how badly the twelve articles of accusation (see pp. 32 and 33) correspond to Joan's words and deeds, as recorded in the register. Her words have been frequently added to, suppressed, or transposed — misquoted, in short, in every possible way. The articles are as far as possible from being, as they should be, "clear and brief, faithfully quoted, and duly co-ordinated."

7. *Joan's Abjuration*

Only one convicted of heresy, i.e., of deliberate error in a matter of faith, stubbornly adhered to, can be legitimately bidden to abjure. Hence Joan was unjustly and impiously called upon to do so. She had no reputation for heresy, except among her mortal enemies, the English. Moreover, her own allegations — that she did not understand the proceedings, and that she acted under coercion and through fear — are sufficient to invalidate the so-called abjuration.

8. *Joan's Relapse*

To what he has already said on this subject (see p. 79) Bréhal adds that in no way known to law can Joan be considered to have relapsed, since far above the level of most women of her condition, she had always been, and remained to the end, an entirely faithful Catholic. In spite of the prolonged and difficult questioning to which she was subjected, "*in none of her answers is she found to have deviated from the Faith.*" A charge of heresy wholly based on her resumption of male clothing is absurd. Her adherence to her revelations "is to be ascribed rather to her credit, not crime; to virtue, not rashness; to religion, not error; to piety, not depravity."

9. *The Interrogatories*

From the record and the witnesses' testimony it is evident that questions were hurled at Joan with such speed and amid such confusion that murmurs of protest were heard from the better disposed assessors; and this badgering continued for months. A man of no mean learning might well have found it hard to reply promptly. The whole proceedings were altogether contrary to canon law, especially in view of Joan's obvious good faith, and lack of learning. Many of the questions were utterly irrelevant, superfluous, and frivolous.

10. *The Assistants*

Joan had no counselor to help her in her answer, though she repeatedly asked for one. Only to manifestly convicted heretics, and especially to the relapsed, should such counsel be denied. (Quicherat, misinterpreting a papal decree, states that counsel was never allowed the accused in a trial for heresy. Can one doubt that our Inquisitor knew his subject better?) False counselors, however, were indeed sent to spy on Joan and ensnare her. The "exhortations" made to her were full of lies, subtleties, artfulness, and confused prolixity. The assessors marshaled against her were partisans of the English, and supported the irrelevancy of the questioning. The two preachers assumed the truth of the lying articles. Even the English nobles should have protested against the preachers' attacks on the King of France, a relative of their own King.

11. *The Findings of the Paris Doctors*

Two judgments based on the articles came from the
Paris faculties of Theology and of Canon Law, respec-
tively. The theologians behaved as though faced with the
utterances of some great heresiarch, condemning Joan's
visions as either fictitious or diabolical. What did they
mean by speaking of "the quality of Joan's person" as one
basis for their censures? Did they refer to her sex, in
spite of Miriam, Anna, Elizabeth, and the most blessed
Virgin herself, all women who prophesied? Or to her race
and parentage, though prophets and apostles were of
humble origin? Or to her life, which was spotless, humble,
and devout? If they had not heard of this, where had
they been hiding? These professors of heavenly wisdom
seemed to ignore the Son of God's condemnation of rash
judgments. "It is better," Bréhal comments, "often to err
by a good opinion of an evil person, than to err less often
by a bad opinion of a good person." Only a madman con-
demns as false philosophical teaching, that is beyond his
comprehension. How much madder to do the same concerning mysterious revelations! Joan was incapable of in-
venting these things, which moreover included true
prophecies and showed the lasting power that lies never
possess. The theory of diabolical origin is contradicted by
Joan's whole way of life. Even though the theologians
were misled by the articles, they should have considered
Joan's rejection of her hostile judge, not to mention the
Poitiers verdict.

The lawyers' findings were more moderate; yet they
accused Joan of severing herself from the unity of the
Church, and of failing to prove her claims by miracles or
from Scripture. Bréhal demolishes the first charge by arguments he has already used; to the second he answers

that the Maid's mission, concerning civil polity, called
for no sign, any more than did Nathan's anointing of Saul
and David. Nevertheless, was it not a miracle that a frail
and simple girl should win such marvelous victories? The
"doctrine" of these doctors should be called cunning
rather than wisdom.

Apparently in order not to embitter the dispute then
raging between the University of Paris and the mendicant
orders, Bréhal ends this chapter by protesting his respect
for the University, and expressing his belief that the professors involved in condemning Joan were few in number.

12. *The Sentence*

The last chapter of the *Recollectio* is based on the argument that a trial so manifestly iniquitous could not pro-
duce a sound verdict. Bréhal, therefore, briefly repeats
most of the charges he has already made concerning the
manner of procedure: Cauchon's lack of jurisdiction, his
bias, Joan's appeal to the Holy See, and so forth. He
again refers to Cauchon's overriding of the assessors' advice at the session of May 29 (see p. 48). "From which it
is evident," he adds, "that such a sentence proceeded, not
from discretion, mother of virtues, but from the stepmother of justice, namely, the deliberate haste of a
vengeful man. It is therefore null." The outrageous
charges contained in the three sentences against Joan
(before her abjuration, just after it, and before her execution) are not supported by her utterances or actions. Nor
was the court's behavior consistent, since Joan was admitted to the sacraments while declared to be under excommunication. The final sentence, moreover, omitted the
required exhortation to seek absolution. Its charge of
heresy was altogether false.

To study the *Recollectio* is to perceive that its condemnation of the Rouen trial is above all based on the prejudiced and inhuman *spirit* which vitiated that process from start to finish. Bréhal does, indeed, lay considerable stress on formal illegalities, but his main argument, supported by countless references to authorities, is directed against the essentially unjust animus which characterized Cauchon's prosecution of Joan. Thus the main theme of this Inquisitor's arraignment is that, since the importance of a trial for heresy itself demands the utmost caution, fairness, honesty, and charity, the Rouen verdict was invalid fundamentally because it was reached by proceedings which violated these requirements in every possible way.

16

REPARATION ACCOMPLISHED

THE papal commissioners, now joined by Longueil, Bishop of Coutances, spent the month of June, 1456, in Paris, making a final study of the whole dossier, including the *Recollectio*. On June 18, they answered a personal plea of Joan's brother, John, with the assurance that definitive action would soon be taken. Before the beginning of July they were again in Rouen, where, after a last declaration of contumacy against those who had been cited to dispute the process, they rendered their verdict at a solemn session on July 7. The Archbishop of Rheims, who presided, read the verdict. There were also present, beside the other commissioners, the promoter of the cause, the advocate and the procurator of the d'Arc family, John d'Arc, and, among numerous clerics, Brother Martin Ladvenu.

The verdict passes in review the successive steps in the rehabilitation: the appointment of the commissioners by the Pope, the plea of Joan's relatives against the Beauvais officials, the articles drawn up against the trial, the inspection of the records, the study of Cardinal d'Estouteville's investigation, the theological memoirs, and the testimony of the witnesses. It confirms the promoter's condemnation of the twelve articles of accusation as fraudulent, calumnious, and malicious; annuls them; and orders them ceremonially torn from the Rouen record. (The remainder of one copy of this record, which had been furnished to the commissioners by the notary Manchon, was presumably also destroyed.)

Reasons for condemning the rest of the trial are then given: the sentences, the quality of the judges, Joan's appeals, the fraud and intimidation by which the so-called abjuration was wrung from her, the judgment of the memorialists on the charges against her. The verdict ends by declaring "the said trials and sentences, tainted with fraud, calumny, injustice, contradiction, and manifest error of law and of fact," to be utterly null and void. Joan is stated to have contracted no stain of infamy therefrom.

The verdict was formally promulgated, in ceremonies accompanied by sermons, on the Place Saint-Ouen, adjacent to the spot where the Maid had "abjured," and on the square of the Old Market, where she had perished, and where a memorial cross was now erected. Similar celebrations took place at Orleans and elsewhere. To Bréhal and Bouillé was assigned the welcome task of journeying to Rome to inform Calixtus III that his mandate had been thoroughly executed.

When conditions permitted, and especially during the last and the present centuries, the most eloquent preachers of France, and sometimes of other countries (Archbishop Ireland of St. Paul was the preacher in 1899), welcomed the privilege of eulogizing Joan from the pulpit of Orleans Cathedral on the annual festival of May 8, commemorating the city's deliverance in 1429. In 1869, the cause of Joan's beatification was introduced, at the plea of the illustrious Bishop of Orleans, Felix Dupanloup. Troubled years ensued, for the Holy See as for France, and it was not until 1909 that Pius X declared the Maid "Blessed." Eleven years later, on May 16, 1920, the frail, clear voice of Benedict XV was raised amid the tense silence of a throng that filled the vast area of St. Peter's. "In honor of the Holy and Undivided Trinity," the Pope proclaimed, "for the exaltation of the Catholic Faith and the growth of the Christian religion, by the authority of Our Lord Jesus Christ, of the blessed Apostles Peter and Paul, and by Our own, after mature deliberation, after offering many prayers to God, after having conferred with Our Venerable Brethren, the Cardinals of the Holy Roman Church, and with the Patriarchs and Bishops present in Rome, We declare that the Blessed Joan of Arc is a Saint, and We inscribe her name in the list of Saints, in the name of the Father, and of the Son, and of the Holy Ghost. Amen."

SANCTA JOANNA
ORA PRO GALLIA
ORA PRO ANGLIA
ORA PRO NOBIS

BIBLIOGRAPHICAL NOTE

THE outstanding collection of source material is Jules Quicherat's *Procès de condamnation et de réhabilitation de Jeanne d'Arc, etc.* (Paris, 1841–49, 5 vols.) It includes all relevant documents available at the time, except that only two theological memoirs are given in full. The hazardous judgments made by Quicherat in his *Aperçus nouveaux sur l'histoire de Jeanne d'Arc* (Paris, 1850) have often been refuted, sometimes with undeserved harshness. They do not affect the greatness of his editorial achievement, which marks an era in the study of Joan's life and trial.

A complete edition of the memoirs, intended as a sixth volume to Quicherat's *magnum opus,* was published by Pierre Lanéry d'Arc, a descendant of Joan's brother, Peter, in 1889. (*Mémoires et consultations en faveur de Jeanne d'Arc par les juges du procès de réhabilitation, etc.,* Paris.) In other respects, besides the inaccuracy of the title, the work leaves something to be desired, but is very valuable as the only available text. Its editor also compiled a vast *Bibliographie . . . des ouvrages relatifs à Jeanne d'Arc,* often referred to by its other title, *Le Livre d'Or de Jeanne d'Arc* (Paris, 1894). As far as publications in French are concerned, it is almost incredibly exhaustive.

Jean Bréhal . . . et la réhabilitation de Jeanne d'Arc, by two Dominican friars, M. J. Belon and François Balme

(Paris, 1893), is a masterpiece of scholarship to which I am deeply indebted. It contains, besides the complete Latin text of the *Recollectio* and a French summary, the best account of the whole rehabilitation. Summaries in French of all the memoirs (except an unimportant one unearthed by Lanéry d'Arc), so ample as to be almost translations, are to be found, amid much controversy, in *La Pucelle devant l'Église de son temps*, by the Jesuit J. B. J. Ayroles (Paris, 1890). This work forms the first volume of the author's colossal *La vraie Jeanne d'Arc* (Paris, 1890–1902).

E. O'Reilly, counselor of the Court of Appeals at Rouen under Napoleon III, published (Paris, 1868) the first French translation of the whole Rouen record and of the rehabilitation testimony (*Les deux procès de condamnation, les enquêtes et la sentence de réhabilitation de Jeanne d'Arc, etc.*), with an excellent introduction, and notes on all the persons involved. The depositions are conveniently arranged according to the portion of Joan's life with which they deal.

Pierre Champion's *Procès de condamnation de Jeanne d'Arc* (Paris, 1920–21, 2 vols.) includes the Latin text of the Rouen record, a French translation, a valuable introduction, and copious notes on the persons. Its only fault is a tendency to follow Quicherat in defending the legality of the trial and belittling the rehabilitation. What amounts to an English translation of Champion's work has been recently made by W. P. Barrett, Coley Taylor, and Ruth H. Kerr (*The Trial of Jeanne d'Arc, etc.*, New York, 1932).

Even in English, the bibliography is enormous. For Joan's military career I have chiefly followed Andrew Lang's admirable, though discursive, study, *The Maid of France* (London and New York, 1908).

APPENDIX A

EXCERPTS FROM BRÉHAL'S RECOLLECTIO

I

On Joan's Answers to Questions About Her Submission to the Church

Est autem in hoc passu maxime consideranda huius puellae simplicitas, quoniam ex satis exiguis parentibus noscitur traducta, et, more campestrium et ruricolarum puellarum, ad pascua dumtaxat post gregem ire, aut aliud qualecumque pauperculum nendi vel suendi artificium docta fuit; ideoque, si ad quaestionem ita arduam et ambiguam non plene respondisset — quemadmodum utique fecit — revera merito digne excusanda venisset. Patet autem eius simplicitas in hac parte, quia, de hac submissione quandoque interrogata, respondit quod, amore Dei, daretur sibi licentia de eundo ad ecclesiam et ad missam. Ecce plane quod ex simplicitate, communi more popularium, maxime intellegebat illud quaesitum de ecclesia materiali et lapidea. Unde et altera vice, dum ei distingueretur ecclesia in militantem et triumphantem, ait: "Videtur mihi quod unum et idem est de Deo et ecclesia, et quod non de hoc debet fieri difficultas." Et subdebat: "Quare facitis vos de hoc difficultatem?"

––––

The simplicity of this girl is very noteworthy in this situation, since she is known to have sprung from quite poor parents, and, like the girls of peasants and farmers,

95

she was taught only to go to the fields after the flock or some other humble art of weaving or sewing. So that, if she had not fully answered such a difficult and ambiguous question — which, however, she did — she would, indeed, have deserved to be excused. But her simplicity is evident in this respect, since, when she was questioned about this submission, she answered that, for the love of God, permission should be given her to go to church and to Mass. In her simplicity, she obviously understood this question, after the manner of the common people, as having to do with the material church of stone. At another time also, when the distinction between the church militant and triumphant was made for her, she said: "It seems to me that it is the same with the Church as with God, and that no difficulty should be made about this." And she added: "Why do you make a difficulty about it?"

II

The English Discover Joan's "Relapse" by Her
Resumption of Male Clothing

Quod attente explorantes illi Anglici alta conclamatione protinus alios complices, mortis Iohannae anhelos, concitarunt, dicentes: "Ecce rea est mortis, vos videritis!" Ad episcopum raptim curritur, assidentium magistratus perquiritur et adducitur, vulgus in diversos et paene contrarios affectus scinditur, gens Anglica quasi ecstatico raptu inebriata circumfertur, vel potius, ut dixerim, effreni vesania corripitur et agitur. At et insons Iohanna venire coram, quasi ad scenicum illusionis spectaculum, compellitur, detruditur, impetitur, et multiplici ludibrio afficienda exponitur. Sed tamen a constantia solita minime dimovetur.

Eagerly investigating this, those Englishmen at once aroused other accomplices, who were panting for Joan's death, and said: "Behold, you shall see she is worthy of death!" They rushed headlong to the bishop, the tribunal of assistants is sought out and fetched, the crowd is torn by different and well-nigh opposite emotions, the English people, as though intoxicated by an ecstatic seizure, is borne hither and thither, or rather is, as it were transported and moved by unbridled madness. But the innocent Joan is also forced, thrust, and driven into their presence, as though to a theatrical spectacle, and exposed to manifold mockery. Nevertheless she is not at all moved from her accustomed constancy.

III

Principles Which Should Have Guided Joan's Judges

Ubi non apparent manifesta indicia de malitia alicuius, debemus eum bonum habere, semper in meliorem partem interpretando quod dubium est. . . . Unde et melius est frequenter falli habendo bonam opinionem de persona mala, quam minus saepe falli habendo malam opinionem de persona bona; quia ex isto fieret iniuria alicui, et non ex primo.

———

Where manifest indications of anyone's malice do not appear, we should consider him good, always interpreting what is doubtful in the better sense. . . . Whence it is better to be often mistaken by holding a good opinion of an evil person than to be less often mistaken by holding a bad opinion of a good person; since the latter does injury to someone, and not the former.

IV

Rashness of the Verdict

Ex quo patet quod huiusmodi sententia, non a discretione, matre virtutum, sed a noverca iustitiae, voluntaria scilicet vindicantis praecipitatione, processit, ideoque nulla est.

———

From which it is evident that a sentence of this sort proceeds, not from discretion, the mother of virtues, but from the stepmother of justice, namely, the voluntary haste of a vengeful man, and is, therefore, null.